CHILLI AND CHOCOLATE

Stars of the Mexican *Cocina*

OTHER TITLES BY ISABEL HOOD

Just the Two of Us – Entertaining Each Other

ISABEL HOOD

CHILLI AND CHOCOLATE

Stars of the Mexican *Cocina*

Illustrations by Philip Hood

Matador
9 De Montfort Mews
Leicester LE1 7FW, UK
Tel: (+44) 116 255 9311 / 9312
Email: books@troubador.co.uk
Web: www.troubador.co.uk/matador

Illustrations © Philip Hood

ISBN 978-1906510-923

A Cataloguing-in-Publication (CIP) catalogue record for this book is available from the British Library.

Typeset in 12pt Palatino by Troubador Publishing Ltd, Leicester, UK
Printed in the UK by TJ International Ltd, Padstow, Cornwall

Matador is an imprint of Troubador Publishing Ltd

To Desmond,
in loving and timeless memory

Viva México

CONTENTS

mi méxico

La Zapoteca

México lindo y querido, si muero lejos de ti... "Beautiful and beloved Mexico, if I die far from thee, let them say that I am merely sleeping, and let them bring me back to thee" goes the traditional song.

I returned recently to my beautiful and beloved Mexico, the enchanted land of my childhood, to celebrate a special wedding anniversary. I had not visited for half a life time, and felt emotional and apprehensive. But I need not have been - my long absence proved to be irrelevant, it was as though I had never been away. I was completely and utterly at home as soon as I set foot once more on Mexican soil.

During the first few days, I just wandered the streets of Mexico City; I revisited old haunts, renewed old friendships, rediscovered my roots, reconnected with people and places; and I kept asking myself the same question over and over again: why, oh why had I not moved heaven and earth throughout my adult life to come back here? And I was overwhelmingly grateful to realise that this haunting, magical country runs so deeply in my veins.

I was just a year old when I arrived in Mexico and therefore steeped in its intensely flavoured, palate-tingling, aromatic cooking from the start. Perhaps that is why my strongest childhood memories revolve around cooking and eating: a kitchen heady with the pungent smell of chilli, onions and fresh coriander; tasty *tortas* stuffed with chicken, refried beans and *guacamole* in my school snack box; rich and deeply flavoured sauces simmering quietly on the stove; dishes of steaming, savoury *enchiladas* or *tacos* for lunch – although it could just as easily be shepherd's pie, and Sunday was always celebrated with roast beef and Yorkshire pudding.

The contents of my snack box were unequivocally Mexican but the school itself was French – 1200 students, both from the French-speaking areas and countries (Africa, French Caribbean, Indochina, Belgium and Switzerland as well as France), and from other parts of the world: Lebanon, Italy, Spain, Austria, Britain, Greece, Russia, Poland and Israel. Some of us were children of expatriates or diplomats, others were second or third generation Mexican "foreigners". Meals at friends' houses were a real adventure and introduced me to pigs' trotters with parsley vinaigrette and *quiche lorraine, moussaka* and *falafel, blinis* dripping with butter, chicken in peanut sauce or cooked in beer, prawns with pineapple or in *paella*, lamb with almonds and prunes, and pasta dishes baked in the oven – and from this kaleidoscope of flavours and experiences, a lifelong love and excitement about food was born. It was, however, many years before it became one of the strongest moving forces in my life.

My father's retirement coincided with the end of my schooling, and when I was in my late teens, the whole family "came home". That had always been the plan. He was British and although he had spent all his adult life in Latin America, he would never have dreamed of ending his days anywhere other than in Britain. So I left my land of luminous skies and rainbows, of snow-capped volcanoes and cascades of scarlet bougainvillea, of dazzling beaches and torrential downpours, and landed in London in July 1968. I knew absolutely nobody. The culture shock was both wildly exhilarating and utterly terrifying. My privileged, sheltered life was turned totally upside down as I learned to travel alone on public transport, explored Carnaby Street, gawped at men dressed in pink velvet bell-bottoms and women drinking beer in pubs. I went to live in a girls' hostel in South Kensington. We were crammed in, three to a room with a basin in the corner and a window looking out over sooty chimneys and grimy rooftops. The sky seemed to be permanently grey and I was unbearably lonely and homesick, lost and adrift in an alien world. I craved sun and light, colour and passion, and most of all, bold, vigorous, aromatic food to ease my aching heart: I longed for the scent of coriander, the fragrance of freshly cooked tortillas, the warmth of chilli, the earthiness of slow-cooked beans flavoured with *chorizo*, the sparkle and richness of an avocado and mango *salsa*, the comfort of a crisp golden *churro* dipped into cinnamon-laced hot chocolate – food memories which I knew even then were bound to haunt me for the rest of my days.

The weekly menu at the hostel was relentlessly grim: cornflakes and sliced white bread; grey meat covered in a glutinous, shiny brown sauce; fish wrapped in a thick, soggy blanket of batter; mushy tinned vegetables; water-logged boiled potatoes which could not even hold their shape. I doubt I tasted a single fresh vegetable or piece of fruit in the whole year I lived there.

When I progressed from the hostel to a shared flat in Earl's Court, I was thrilled to have a kitchen at my disposal and although I had never been taught to cook, I had spent countless childhood hours watching Juana and then Carmen preparing the family meals. But sadly, MacFisheries Supermarket in the Earl's Court Road proved somewhat inadequate when it came to providing the ingredients for *tacos* and *tingas*, and Mexico and the memory of its glorious dishes slowly faded from my life. My passion for food also faded as I followed the example of successive flatmates and learned to live on staples like tinned tomato soup, Vesta packets and TV dinners.

It was not until my early thirties that I managed to switch to a different set of tracks. Disenchanted and utterly frustrated with all aspects of my existence, I first took a good hard look at where I was and then some ridiculously overdue decisions about where I wanted to go and what I wanted to do with my future. And suddenly my slumbering passion sprang to life again, its splendour and strength undimmed by its long exile, and I found myself pushed inexorably in a very specific direction. I could not resist. I saved up for a year, trained as a chef, eventually started up my own catering business and, twenty five years later, food and cooking are tightly woven into the very fabric of my life.

There is no MacFisheries nowadays in the Earl's Court Road, and while thirty five years ago corn tortillas in tins were pretty much the extent of the Mexican ingredients available, now I can buy huge bunches of fresh coriander at my local supermarket, as well as fresh chillies, beans, *masa harina* and *chorizo* sausages. Specialist chillies, both fresh and dried, corn husks for *tamales*, even *tomatillos* can be bought by mail order. And so, at long last, I can recreate at will the flavours of my childhood and the fabulous dishes which Juana and Carmen used to make; and I can reconnect effortlessly with *mi tierra*, my native soil, through its food.

Mexico is a land of jagged mountain peaks, near-deserts, rain forests, jungles and swamps – of diverse climates, terrains and peoples. The roots of its cuisine reach deep down into its ancient cultures and indigenous ingredients. Cortés and his conquering army were amazed by the unfamiliar foods they found: potatoes and tomatoes, chillies and peppers, squashes and pumpkins, avocadoes and pineapples, vanilla and chocolate, a multitude of crops which were totally unknown in Europe. Turkeys, quail and plump little dogs bred specially for the table were cooked in intensely flavoured sauces thickened with seeds and nuts; beans of different colours – black, red, yellow, tan, speckled - simmered in cooking pots in the market places; corn dumplings wrapped in corn husks were steamed in underground pits and crushed corn was mixed with lime and made into fragrant pancakes, often more than a foot in diameter. There were few domesticated animals: no chickens or their nutritious eggs, no cattle and therefore no milk, butter or cheese; and most importantly, no pigs, and therefore no cooking fat – boiling, steaming and baking on a hot griddle were the main methods of cooking. With the arrival of the pig and its rich, tasty lard, frying became possible and this is still one of the cornerstones of true Mexican cooking. The Spaniards also introduced other modern Mexican staples like onions and garlic, rice, and spices; a touch of European sophistication was added to the cuisine during the short reign of the Emperor Maximilian, and immigrants over the years brought new foodstuffs; but the heart and soul of Mexican food today remains Aztec and Toltec, Zapotec, Olmec and Mayan, in spite of the strong Spanish influence. It is a bold, earthy, exciting and deeply satisfying cuisine, a *cocina* whose flavours are sparkling and energising - warm and fruity, sharp and zesty - rich and complex, with countless hidden layers.

And yet, Mexican food seems to be very underrated outside America. The main reason, I suspect, is because our experience of it is mainly limited to *nachos* and bottled *salsas*, *taco* shells and *fajitas*, Chiquitos and Old El Paso. But these are no more representative of real Mexican food than a tin of spaghetti hoops is of Italian food. They are nothing but dull sparks in a galaxy of bright and shining stars. Another important reason is probably that many of the ingredients appear intimidating. We are used to avocadoes, but a dark, sultry, highly aromatic dried chilli is a different matter. Grinding cumin and fresh coriander seeds for a curry is commonplace, but grinding bright pink annatto seeds with garlic and vinegar for a *pibil* marinade is not quite the same thing. Sea bass is easily wrapped in a foil parcel ready for baking, while making an envelope out of corn husks is far from familiar… Many traditional Mexican dishes also require effort and time in the kitchen, which often does not fit in with a 21st century lifestyle and the increasingly 'fast-food' approach to cooking. But a foray into real Mexican food always proves infinitely rewarding and I hope that this book will encourage readers to venture into a fascinating, nourishing, sometimes mysterious, always bewitching, area of gastronomy.

However, this book is not about "traditional" or "authentic" Mexican food! I am not yet sufficiently qualified to write about it in that way. It is about Mexican food as I remember it; it is about my deeply personal, very nostalgic, journey back to the food of my childhood; and it is also about my understanding and modern interpretation of Mexican food. I have structured the book around five specific foods which, for me, represent the very heart of Mexico's glorious cuisine, its quintessential, dominant ingredients and flavours. Many will disagree with me, but then this is **my** Mexican food, **my** Mexico, *mi México lindo y querido*, the Mexico which comes alive in my kitchen every time I prepare a tomato *salsa*, scented with fresh coriander and heady with chilli; or a *mole*, deep and rich with chocolate and spices; or a simple dish of black beans flavoured with cumin and bacon. As I cook and breathe in the intoxicating aromas, I can close my eyes and be instantly transported to the little street stall by the bus station in Tuxtla Gutíerrez where we bought *tortas* filled with *huevos a la mexicana* just before dawn; or to a *fonda* in Guanajuato – just three rickety tables under a tattered awning and a memorable *quesadilla* of *chorizo* and strips of *poblano* chilli; or the courtyard garden of the old colonial palace in Mérida where we ate a simple roast chicken with a mango and avocado *salsa* under a jacaranda tree in full bloom. And as, in my mind's eye, I wander along the aisles of the indoor market in Oaxaca, past huge woven baskets of dried chillies and piles of plantains, papayas and guavas, I hear the *marchantas*, the stall holders, calling out to me: "*que se va llevar, que se va llevar*", "what will you take, what will you take".

El Águila y La Serpiente

NOTES ON THE RECIPES

Do not mix metric and imperial measures. Follow one set only.

All spoon measurements are level unless otherwise stated: 1 tsp = 5 ml; 1 tbsp = 15 ml.

Eggs are large unless otherwise stated. If you use a different size, adjust the amount of liquid added to obtain the right consistency.

Always wash, peel, core and seed, if necessary, fresh foods before use. Ensure that all produce is as fresh as possible and in good condition.

Seasoning and the use of strongly flavoured ingredients, such as onions, garlic and chillies, are very much a matter of personal taste. Taste the food you cook and adjust seasoning and heat to suit your own taste. Unless a particular type or heat of fresh chilli is specified in the recipe, use as mild or hot a chilli as you like; and if the finished dish is not hot and spicy enough for you, feel free to increase the quantity of chillies or the amount of chilli sauce.

The flavour of spices such as cumin and coriander is more intense and aromatic if whole seeds are used and freshly ground. Whole seeds are therefore specified in the recipes. Feel free to substitute commercially ground spices if you are unable to grind your own, but the result will not be quite as good!

Tin and packet sizes are approximate and will depend on the particular brand.

All ovens vary, so cooking times have to be approximate. Adjust cooking times and temperatures according to manufacturers' instructions.

Always use fresh herbs unless dried are specifically called for. If it is necessary to substitute dried herbs for fresh, use half the quantity stated. Chopped frozen varieties are much better than dried. There is no substitute for fresh parsley and coriander.

Always preheat the oven and cook on the middle shelf unless otherwise specified.

earth

Cazuela de frijoles

They simmer quietly for hours on a backburner. They may be plain, flavoured with nothing more than a chopped onion, a sprig of the native herb, *epazote,* and a bay leaf; or they may be richly perfumed with spicy *chorizo,* roasted tomatoes and a purée of dark, dried chillies. Their texture is creamy and smooth, their broth thick and nourishing, their fragrance warm and comforting. They are utterly earthy – true Mexican food for the soul, wholesome, soothing, satisfying. No Mexican kitchen is ever without its bubbling earthenware *cazuela* of *frijoles* – beans are an integral part of everyday life and food.

My childhood weekend breakfasts always featured *frijoles,* as well as a spicy egg dish like Country Eggs, perhaps a spoonful of savoury tortilla casserole, a cup of steaming hot chocolate redolent with cinnamon… No 'cooked breakfast' could ever compare. *Frijoles* are still one of my favourite foods and there is always a pot of them in my refrigerator, ready to be reheated for a quick and easy lunch; or to be fried and mashed up with onions, bacon and spices and eaten with tortilla chips or on toast; or to be added to a salad or vegetable soup. They are wonderfully versatile and adaptable, and although they take time to cook and therefore need forward planning, they require little attention and are content to be left alone for hours on end until they stew to a luscious softness.

A stroll through any Mexican market will take you past huge woven baskets of beans in a wonderful range of earthy hues – from shiny black to creamy white and all manner of pinks, reds, golds and russets in between. There are countless varieties and the colour changes with the region, starting off pale in the North and growing progressively darker on the way South. Stop to eat at a market *fonda* or a street stall, and you are bound to be served beans in one form or another with everything: refried and piled onto *tostadas* or stuffed into large chillies, spooned over scrambled eggs, in a *taco* or *enchilada,* spread in *tortas,* stirred into rich *moles* and *tingas* – and however they are done, they will be utterly delicious and utterly Mexican.

Although beans all have their own nuance of flavour and texture, they are in most cases interchangeable. However, I have in some instances detailed a specific type of bean, either because I feel it is more appropriate, or because it is regional and therefore essential to the personality of an individual dish.

Lentils and chickpeas are not native to the Americas but, having arrived with the Spaniards, they rapidly made themselves at home and feature frequently in regional cuisines, particularly cooked with fruit or rice. I personally find that they lack the gorgeous earthiness of beans, their reassurance and richness, but they work well with true Mexican ingredients, so I have included some recipes.

All pulses have one drawback, and that is that they can be notoriously difficult to digest! Soaking them and then cooking them in fresh water is supposed to deal with this problem, but in my experience, it makes no difference and there is a loss of flavour and texture. Mexican cooks do not soak beans: they do, however, often add *epazote* and this does indeed make a very considerable difference. Nevertheless, *epazote*, although easy to grow, is hard to find (see Resources). A strip of kombu seaweed and bay leaves are both good alternatives, but the best solution I have found is to cook the beans for a long time, a good couple of hours at least.

BASIC BEANS
Frijoles de Olla

These simple beans are eaten by virtually every Mexican at least once a day and, together with corn, are an essential source of protein for the many who cannot afford meat. There is virtually no preparation involved and all they need is to be allowed to cook undisturbed for several hours, by which time they will be soft, thick and irresistibly earthy. They will keep in the refrigerator for days and are an excellent stand-by, as they can be made into a quick and satisfying meal with very little effort.

Serves 6

500 g/18 oz beans, black, red kidney, haricot or pinto
200 g/7 oz onions, peeled and finely sliced
3 garlic cloves, peeled
1 bay leaf
60 ml/4 tbsp olive oil
Warm tortillas, bread or cooked rice, to serve (optional)
Sea salt and freshly ground black pepper

Place the beans in a colander and rinse them under cold, running water. Put them in a large saucepan with the onions, garlic and bay leaf, add enough water to cover by 10 cm/4 in, and bring to the boil over medium heat. Turn the heat down to low, cover the saucepan and simmer very gently for at least 2 hours, preferably 3 or 4, until the beans are totally tender. Check them every now and then to make sure that they are not drying out and are covered by at least 1 cm/½ in of water. Add some seasoning and cook for another 20 minutes. Stir in the olive oil just before serving.

Serve in warm, deep bowls with tortillas, bread or rice.

RED BEAN SOUP
Sopa de Frijol

There are countless variations of bean soup throughout the country, made with whatever beans and chillies are grown locally, and it never fails to satisfy. In the state of Michoacán, it is called *Sopa Tarasca* or *Purépecha* after the pre-Hispanic Tarasca civilisation which was renowned for its beautiful metal work. We travelled from the sultry, flower-scented Pacific coast up into the Sierra Madre mountains of Michoacán and the little town of Pátzcuaro, on the shores of a picture postcard lake. The contrast could not have been greater as we exchanged brilliant sunshine and tropical warmth for leaden skies and a steady cold drizzle! First port of call was the *zócalo* with its handsome colonial mansions and arcades, and La Surtidora, whose menu proudly boasts that it was established in 1923 and has specialised in local dishes ever since. *Sopa Tarasca* was just what we needed after our long bus journey, and the waiter was delighted to tell us all about it; he maintained that it is traditionally made with milk and butter, but despite subsequent enquiries at the market *fondas* and considerable research, I have not found a recipe to support his assurances.

This soup is a meal in itself – deeply nourishing, richly spiced, savoury with cheese and sharp with soured cream or yoghurt. If you want to serve it as a first course, follow it with something fairly light like Yucatecan Marinated Salmon with Guacamole (page 180).

Serves 4

½ x quantity Basic Beans, made with red kidney beans (page 11)
750 g/1 ¾ lb tomatoes, halved
2 garlic cloves, unpeeled
2 medium hot green chillies
60 ml/4 tbsp olive oil
250 g/9 oz onions, peeled and coarsely chopped
1 ½ tsp cumin seeds, ground medium fine in a mortar or spice grinder
200 ml/7 fl oz soured cream or Greek-style plain yoghurt
200 g/7 oz Feta cheese

150 g/5 oz plain tortilla chips
15 g/½ oz fresh coriander, coarsely chopped
Sea salt and freshly ground black pepper

Remove the bay leaf from the beans and process them with their cooking liquid in a food processor until fairly smooth. Set aside.

Heat the grill to high. Arrange the tomatoes, cut side up, garlic and chillies on a roasting tray lined with foil and grill them 10 cm/4 in from the heat for 10 minutes. Turn the garlic and chillies over and grill for another 10 minutes – by then they should be soft and brown, and the tomatoes lightly charred. Cool slightly, then peel the garlic; halve the chillies and scrape out and discard the seeds. Put the garlic and chillies in a food processor, add the tomatoes and all their juices, and blend to a coarse purée.

While the vegetables are grilling, heat the olive oil in a large saucepan and add the onions. Cook on medium heat, stirring occasionally, until lightly browned, about 15 minutes. Sprinkle on the cumin and some seasoning, and cook for a further 5 minutes. Add the tomato purée and stir-fry over high heat until thick. Stir in the beans, add enough water to make it the consistency of double cream, and simmer, stirring occasionally, for 20 minutes. Check the seasoning.

Ladle the soup into warm bowls and top with a spoonful of soured cream or yoghurt, some crumbled Feta cheese, a handful of tortilla chips and the fresh coriander.

Serve immediately.

PUMPKIN SOUP WITH BEANS AND SALSA
Sopa de Calabaza

Pumpkins and squashes of all types are native to the Americas and feature abundantly in markets and vegetable dishes throughout the autumn. Their flavour is not pronounced and they benefit from being stewed or roasted until they almost start to caramelise, thereby strengthening their sweetness and richness. This same sweetness cries out for sharp, acid tastes like lemon, tomatoes and soured cream.

Variations of this soup were being dished up throughout the noisy, crowded central market in Cholula, often flamboyantly garnished with fresh courgette flowers, either whole or torn into strips and lightly steamed. Each cook added her own little touch, and having sampled the soup at three different stalls, we were subsequently deeply disappointed by the one we were served at a rather slick and expensive restaurant – pale, heavy with cream and decidedly bland, *"sopa de turista"*, soup for the tourists.

You can use any kind of bean – black beans in particular contrast colourfully with the bright orange soup, but I prefer the seductive, creamy softness of pinto beans. And if you have neither cooked beans to hand nor the time to cook them from scratch, tinned red kidney beans will do.

Serves 4

15 ml/1 tablespoon olive oil
150 g/5 oz onions, peeled and coarsely chopped
1.5 kg/3 lb pumpkin or butternut squash, peeled, deseeded and cubed
1 ½ cups cooked beans, drained
Fresh lemon juice
1 x quantity Raw Tomato Salsa (page 201)
Soured cream or Greek-style plain yoghurt
Sea salt and freshly ground black pepper

Heat the olive oil in a medium saucepan and add the onions. Cook, stirring occasionally, until translucent, about 10 minutes – just long enough in fact to prepare the pumpkin. Stir in the pumpkin and some seasoning, cover the pan, turn the heat right down and leave to stew gently until totally soft and starting to brown, about 30 minutes. Stir it every now and then, scraping the bottom of the pan well, to make sure it is not sticking and burning.

Add enough water to cover the pumpkin, turn the heat up to medium, bring to the boil and simmer for 10 minutes. Allow to cool slightly before puréeing in a blender or food processor. Pour back into the saucepan and add enough water to make it the consistency of double cream. Add the beans and bring to the boil. Check the seasoning and add some lemon juice if it is too cloying, but only enough to cut the sweetness as the salsa and soured cream or yoghurt will add more acidity – it all depends on the pumpkin, and one of the soup's many charms is the sweet and sharp contrast.

Ladle the soup into four warm bowls, add a good dollop of salsa, drizzle it all with some soured cream or yoghurt and serve immediately.

REFRIED BEANS
Frijoles Refritos

Fried beans would be a more appropriate description, as they are only fried once. The prefix *"re"* in Mexico is used for emphasis, as in *"re bueno"*, really good, or *"re bonita"*, so pretty. When it comes to these beans, the *"re"* would be better translated as "well" fried. They are often used as an accompaniment, invariably sitting beside eggs at breakfast or *tacos* at lunchtime, garnished with a crown of spiky tortilla chips. But they are also delicious on their own, simply wrapped in a warm tortilla, and particularly come into their own as a filling, a base or a topping, as in *tortas, tostadas* and *tacos*.

Serves 6

60 ml/4 tbsp olive oil
100 g/4 oz onions, peeled and coarsely chopped
1 mild red or green chilli, deseeded and finely sliced
1 garlic clove, peeled and sliced
1 x quantity Basic Beans (page 11)
1 tsp cumin seeds, coarsely ground in a mortar or spice grinder
Sea salt and freshly ground black pepper

Heat half the oil in a small saucepan and cook the onions, chilli and garlic gently until soft and lightly browned, about 15 minutes.

Remove the bay leaf from the beans, place them with their liquid in a food processor, add the onion mixture, cumin and some seasoning, and blend until you have a chunky paste.

Heat the remaining olive oil in a heavy frying pan, add the bean purée and cook over gentle heat for about 15 minutes, stirring occasionally – it should be fairly thick, without any hint of sloppiness. Check the seasoning.

These beans keep well in the refrigerator but be sure to add a bit of water when you reheat them or they will be very solid.

BEANS ON TOAST
Molletes a la Mexicana

Molletes are a popular breakfast dish, much favoured by business men by the looks of it. Breakfast meetings are commonplace, and whenever we were staying in a city such as Mexico, Mérida or Morelia and eating in a hotel restaurant or café, there were invariably several tables of business men, impeccable in their suits and ties, mobile phones at the ready, setting themselves up for the day with a plate of savoury, sustaining *molletes*. It is a wonderful combination of flavours and textures: crisp bread, rich, soft beans, pungent cheese, fresh salsa sparkling with chillies and herbs. A torpedo-shaped crisp roll called *bolillo* is used in Mexico, and is roughly the size of a small hand. *Ciabatta* rolls or *petits pains* are a good substitute.

Serves 2/4

Crisp bread rolls – 2 ciabatta rolls or 4 petits pains
½ x quantity Refried Beans (page 16)
100 g/4 oz Farmhouse Cheddar cheese, coarsely grated
½ x quantity Raw Tomato Salsa (page 201)

Split the rolls and toast the cut side lightly. Place them toasted side up on a baking tray lined with foil and spread the beans over them. Top with the cheese.

Heat the grill to high. Grill the rolls, about 10 cm/4 in from the heat, until the cheese has melted and is starting to bubble.

Place the molletes on two warm plates, spoon some of the salsa over them, and serve immediately, with extra salsa on the side.

BEANS IN RED MOLE SAUCE
Frijoles en Mole Rojo

Faintly reminiscent of Boston Baked Beans, these beans are rich, sultry and boldly flavoured, real pre-Hispanic Mexican food. I love them for breakfast with scrambled egg dishes like *Migas* (page 55), but I have to admit that some people might find them over the top first thing in the morning! Like classic *moles*, they go well with fruit so if you are having them for supper, Rice with Plantains (page 250) and Crunchy Fruity Salad (page 252) are good accompaniments, as are Mexican Salad (page 210) and warm tortillas.

The *tahini* is far from authentic but much easier than toasting and grinding sesame seeds, and the fundamental flavour is not affected.

Serves 8

100 g/4 oz mulato chillies (see Resources)
25 g/1 oz guajillo chillies (see Resources)
1 x quantity Grilled Tomato Sauce (page 204)
1 tsp ground cinnamon
1 tbsp dried Mexican oregano (see Resources)
30 g/1 ¼ oz dark tahini (sesame paste)
30 g/1 ¼ oz dark chocolate (minimum 70% cocoa solids), coarsely chopped
1 to 2 tbsp runny honey
1 x quantity Basic Beans, made with haricot beans (page 11)
Sea salt and freshly ground black pepper

Heat a heavy frying pan over medium heat and toast the chillies, pressing down on them with a spatula, until they start to smell aromatic, about 3 minutes. Flip them over and do the same on the other side. Place them in a bowl, cover with boiling water, put a small saucepan lid or plate on top to keep them submerged, and set them aside to soak for 30 minutes. Drain them, and remove the stalks, seeds and ribs. Place them in a food processor, add about 100 ml/3 ½ fl oz of water and process until you have a thick, smooth sauce. Strain through a medium mesh strainer to remove the bits of skin.

Bring the tomato sauce to the boil in a large frying pan and add the chilli purée. Cook, stirring occasionally, for 15 minutes. Stir in the cinnamon, oregano, tahini, chocolate, 1 tbsp of honey and some seasoning, and simmer for a further 10 minutes. Pour in the beans and their cooking liquid, bring back to the boil, turn the heat right down and leave to cook for about 30 minutes, giving them a stir every now and then, until the sauce is thick and the beans well coated – the beans will absorb the wonderful flavours of the sauce.

Check the seasoning and add a bit more honey if needed; you are looking for a mellow sauce, not a sweet one, and the amount of honey will depend on the acidity of the tomatoes.

Serve immediately in deep warm bowls.

TORTILLAS IN BEAN SAUCE
Enfrijoladas

Rather like *chilaquiles* (page 36) and *enjitomatadas* (page 82), *enfrijoladas* are poverty cuisine, at its most satisfying and comforting – the ingredients are cheap and plentiful, staples to be found under every shabby market awning and in every Mexican household, particularly the pot of beans, which is always simmering away somewhere in the kitchen. The flavours are deep and rich with earthy *frijoles*, cheese and cream, and yet sparkling and fresh with the spicy *salsa* and *guacamole*. They are eaten mostly for breakfast, predominantly at street stalls and market *fondas*, as cooking them does not require much in the way of equipment – they are on the whole a one pot meal, easy to rustle up on a single gas burner or a little stove full of glowing coals on the pavement. Whole stale corn tortillas are normally used; they are dipped into the sauce one by one, folded over like crêpes Suzette and piled neatly on one side of the pan – the street cooks' dexterity is a joy to watch as they deftly flip them this way and that like a master chef. However, tortilla chips make the whole process much simpler if less authentic, and their crunch, once softened by the sauce, gives them a wonderful chewy texture. Be generous with the chillies in the *salsa*, as their warmth and shimmer are essential to the liveliness of the overall dish.

Serves 4

½ x quantity Basic Beans, made with black or red kidney beans (page 11)
1 tbsp olive oil
150 g/5 oz onions, peeled and coarsely chopped
2 garlic cloves, peeled and crushed
1 tbsp cumin seeds, coarsely ground in a mortar or spice grinder
1 tbsp dried Mexican oregano (see Resources)
250 g/9 oz plain tortilla chips
150 g/5 oz Farmhouse Cheddar cheese, coarsely grated
250 ml/8 fl oz soured cream or Greek-style plain yoghurt
1 x quantity Raw Tomato Salsa (page 201)
1 x quantity Guacamole without tomatoes (page 159)
Sea salt and freshly ground black pepper

Remove the bay leaf from the beans and purée them with their liquid in a food processor until fairly smooth, adding a bit of water if the mixture is very thick – it needs to be of a pouring consistency, as it will thicken when the tortillas are added.

Heat the oven to its lowest temperature and put a large, deep serving dish to warm.

Heat the olive oil in a large frying pan, add the onions, garlic, cumin seeds, oregano and a bit of seasoning, and cook gently, stirring occasionally, until soft and starting to brown. Add the bean purée and bring to the boil, stirring all the time, as it tends to stick instantly to the bottom of the pan. Check the seasoning, leaving it just a bit on the bland side, as tortilla chips are salty. Stir in the tortilla chips, turning them over and over in the sauce with a large spoon until they are well coated.

Spoon the *enfrijoladas* into the warm serving dish. Drizzle the soured cream or yoghurt over them, sprinkle with the cheese, and top with the salsa. Serve immediately with the guacamole and any remaining salsa on the side.

Quetzalcoatl, serpiente emplumada

EGGS FROM MORELIA
Huevos Morelianos

The state of Michoacán is justly renowned for its glorious food and its capital, Morelia, now a UNESCO World Cultural Heritage site, is a jewel of a colonial city, so much so that we found it almost more Spanish than Mexican, with its open air cafés, leafy squares and designer shops. The restaurant of the Hotel Casino, under the arcades of one of the 17th century mansions surrounding the central Plaza de Armas, seems determined to hold on to its Mexican identity by stating on its menu that it serves only authentic Michoacán specialities. These specialities lose much of their charm from excessive and pointless garnishes and a rather heavy-handed attempt at sophistication, but their Morelian eggs are delicious, a perfect mid-morning breakfast, especially if accompanied by a plate of fresh guavas – October is the time for them in Michoacán – and a large cup of frothy "pre-Hispanic" chocolate.

Serves 2

For the bean sauce:-
1 tbsp olive oil
150 g/5 oz onions, peeled and coarsely chopped
2 garlic cloves, peeled and crushed
1 tbsp cumin seeds, coarsely ground in a mortar or spice grinder
1 tbsp dried Mexican oregano (see Resources)
½ x quantity Basic Beans, made with black or red kidney beans (page 11)
Sea salt and freshly ground black pepper

For the eggs:-
1 tbsp olive oil
50 g/2 oz onions, peeled and coarsely chopped
1 garlic clove, peeled and crushed
1 hot red or green chilli, deseeded and finely chopped
100 g/4 oz tomatoes, coarsely chopped
4 eggs, beaten
Sea salt and freshly ground black pepper

To serve:-
4 corn tortillas, warmed
120 ml/4 fl oz soured cream or Greek-style plain yoghurt
100 g/4 oz Farmhouse Cheddar cheese, coarsely grated
15 g/½ oz fresh coriander, coarsely chopped

To prepare the bean sauce, heat the olive oil in a small frying pan, add the onions and garlic, and cook over medium heat, stirring now and then, until golden, about 15 minutes. Add the cumin and oregano and stir-fry for a further 5 minutes.

Remove the bay leaf from the beans and purée them with their liquid and the onion mixture in a food processor until fairly smooth, adding a bit of water if the mixture is very thick – it needs to be the consistency of double cream. Reheat before serving.

For the eggs, heat the oil in a small saucepan and add the onions, garlic and chilli. Cook gently until softened, about 10 minutes. Stir in the tomatoes and some seasoning, and continue to cook, stirring occasionally, until most of the moisture has evaporated. Pour in the beaten eggs and cook, stirring constantly, until softly scrambled.

Place the tortillas on two warm plates, divide the scrambled eggs between them, and fold them over to enclose the filling. Pour the bean sauce over them, drizzle with soured cream or yoghurt and sprinkle with cheese and coriander.

Serve immediately.

BEAN MASH
Puré de Frijol

The rich, earthy texture of mashed beans is incredibly satisfying and cannot be achieved with any real degree of success by using tinned beans, but if you are pushed for time, a tin of haricot beans will do. Avoid tinned pinto beans as they always seem to have a slight but unpleasant metallic taste. This *puré* is a simpler, lighter version of Refried Beans (page 16), and tends to keeps its place well in the background, offering support to a more flamboyant and strongly flavoured partner rather than taking centre stage. However, it is also delicious on its own, soothing and mellow, with tortillas or bread.

Serves 6

1 x quantity Basic Beans, made with pinto or haricot beans (page 11)
200 ml/7 fl oz olive oil
Warm tortillas or bread, to serve (optional)
Sea salt and freshly ground black pepper

Remove the bay leaf from the beans and spoon them into a food processor, leaving most of their liquid behind. Pour in the olive oil and process until quite smooth, adding more of the cooking liquid if necessary. Reheat gently in a frying pan or a basin over boiling water. Check the seasoning after reheating.

Serve immediately with warm tortillas or bread.

CARIBBEAN BEANS
Frijoles del Caribe

This deliciously unctuous bean dish is very reminiscent of the cuisine of Cuba and its "black beans and rice", which is hardly surprising as the first *Conquistadores* to arrive in the southern state of Yucatán, led by Hernández de Córdoba, had set sail from Cuba. They were driven back into the sea at Campeche by the Mayan warriors in 1517, but they were followed by others and eventually the Mayan people were subjugated. Black beans feature extensively in the local cooking, and the presence of the fiery *habañero* chilli makes the dish unequivocally Yucatecan. The fried plantains, coconut and tropical fruit salsa give it a decidedly southern slant, and these rich, spicy, exotic *frijoles* are served all along the Caribbean coast of the Yucatán peninsula. Warm corn tortillas or rice are the standard accompaniment.

Serves 4

2 tbsp olive oil
275 g/10 oz onions, peeled and coarsely chopped
3 garlic cloves, peeled and crushed
1 tbsp cumin seeds, coarsely ground in a mortar or spice grinder
1 x quantity Basic Beans, made with black beans (page 11)
1 dried habañero chilli (see Resources)
2 large ripe plantains, about 250 g/9 oz each, peeled and cut into 1 cm/ ½ in rounds
250 g/9 oz creamed coconut
Sea salt and freshly ground black pepper

1 x quantity Avocado and Mango Salsa (page 185)

Heat 1 tbsp of the olive oil in a large saucepan, add the onions, garlic and some seasoning, and cook gently, stirring occasionally, until soft and just starting to brown, about 20 minutes. Add the cumin and cook for a further 5 minutes. Pour in the beans and their cooking liquid and bring to the boil. Push the chilli down into the beans, cover the pan and simmer for 30 minutes.

Heat the grill to its highest setting and the oven to its lowest setting. Line the grill pan with foil, arrange the plantain slices on it, and brush them with some of the remaining olive oil. Grill them 5 cm/2 in from the heat until golden, then carefully turn them over and do the same on the other side. Transfer to the oven and keep warm until ready to serve.

Stir the coconut cream into the beans and let it melt. Fish out and discard the habañero chilli (it is VERY hot!), and check the seasoning.

To serve, divide the beans between four warm plates and top first with the plantain slices and then a good spoonful of salsa, adding more salsa as you eat.

COWBOY BEANS
Frijoles del Charro

These beans are a speciality of the cattle country of Northern Mexico and named after its horsemen, the *charros*. The *charros* are a wonderful sight, dressed in fancy black suits all embroidered with gold thread, and huge wide-brimmed hats, nonchalantly at ease on their tooled leather saddles. If you want to be authentic, use the bright red *chorizo* fat rather than olive oil – the flavour will be wonderful but your arteries may suffer! In the absence of *poblano* chillies, substitute green peppers and a couple of mild green chillies.

Serves 8

350 g/12 oz poblano chillies (see Resources) or green peppers and 2 mild
green chillies
300 g/11 oz tomatoes
150 g/5 oz chorizo sausage, diced
45 ml/3 tbsp olive oil
200 g/7 oz onions, peeled and coarsely chopped
2 garlic cloves, peeled and crushed
1 tsp Mexican dried oregano (see Resources)
1 x quantity Basic Beans, made with pinto beans (page 11)
15 g/½ oz fresh coriander, coarsely chopped
Sea salt and freshly ground black pepper
Cooked rice or warm tortillas, to serve

Heat the grill to high. Line the grill pan with foil and arrange the chillies and tomatoes on it. Grill them, about 10 cm/4 in from the heat, until lightly charred and softened on one side, then turn them over and do the same on the other side. Cool for about 10 minutes, then chop the tomatoes coarsely, reserving any juices. Peel the chillies, discard the seeds, and cut the flesh into strips.

While the tomatoes and chillies are grilling, cook the chorizo in a large heavy saucepan over medium heat, stirring every so often, until it has released most of its fat and is golden, about 10 minutes. With a slotted spoon, remove it to a plate lined with kitchen paper to drain. Discard the fat and wipe out the pan. Return it to the heat, add the olive oil, onions and garlic, and cook gently until soft and golden, about 20 minutes. Stir in the chorizo, tomatoes, chillies, oregano and beans with their liquid, season well, and cook over gentle heat for about 45 minutes, to blend the flavours.

Sprinkle with coriander and serve immediately with rice or tortillas.

Maguey

POTATO WEDGE *NACHOS*

Nachos are often Mexican food at its worst, even in Mexico, let alone in Mexican restaurants abroad. We tried them just once, at a restaurant by the Mayan ruins of Palenque, and they were quite awful: bright orange, processed, greasy cheese, soggy tortilla chips, runny beans, bottled *salsa* instead of *guacamole* – real tourist food. However, at their best, made with care and proper ingredients, they are utterly delicious. I often use potatoes instead of tortilla chips to make *nachos* into a substantial supper dish. Jars of sharp, vinegary *jalapeño* chillies are available in the "world foods" section of most supermarkets. Although it sounds like an awful lot of potatoes, they shrink very considerably during roasting and if you make any less, you will feel decidedly cheated!

Serves 2

700 g/1 ½ lb potatoes, scrubbed
45 ml/3 tbsp olive oil
1 x quantity Refried Beans (page 16)
125 g/4 ½ oz Farmhouse Cheddar cheese, coarsely grated
15 g/½ oz fresh coriander, coarsely chopped
4 pickled jalapeño chillies
1 x quantity Guacamole (page 159)
Sea salt and freshly ground black pepper

Heat the oven to 220°C/425°F/gas 7/fan oven 200°C.

Cut the potatoes into finger-sized wedges and cook them in boiling salted water for 5 minutes. Drain them, place them in a baking dish which holds them fairly snugly, drizzle with 45 ml/3 tbsp of olive oil, season and stir well to coat. Cook in the oven for about 45 minutes, stirring every now and then, until they are nice and crusty.

Spoon the beans over the potatoes and top with the grated cheese. Return to the oven for ten minutes, until the beans are hot and the cheese melted and gooey. Sprinkle on fresh coriander.
Serve with guacamole sauce & pickled jalapenos.

Sprinkle with coriander and serve immediately with pickled jalapeño chillies and guacamole.

BEAN AND PUMPKIN SEED SALAD
Frijoles en Vinagreta de Pepita

Butter beans work particularly well in this salad, as the darker coloured ones tend to make it look rather dull. It is a fresh and substantial lunch dish, with some tortillas or some bread, and a lovely and unusual addition to a buffet, making a welcome change from the normal bean salads. Pumpkin seeds, *pepitas,* are a staple ingredient in Mexico. Along with sesame seeds, they were used to thicken sauces in pre-Hispanic times, and make an appearance in countless dishes, from *moles* to vegetable dishes and salads, and as a popular street snack, toasted with salt on a griddle and sold in paper cones. Their oil is highly, and rightly, prized, khaki green and richly nutty.

Serves 2

150 g/5 oz hulled pumpkin seeds
350 g/12 oz tomatoes, halved
2 garlic cloves, peeled
75 g/3 oz red onions, peeled and coarsely chopped
60 ml/4 tbsp olive oil
Fresh lemon juice
1 tsp chipotle chilli sauce (see Resources)
15 g/½ oz fresh coriander + a good handful of leaves
2 x 400 g/14 oz tins butter beans, rinsed and drained
100 g/4 oz cherry tomatoes, quartered
Sea salt and freshly ground black pepper

Heat the oven to 160°C/325°F/gas 3/fan oven 145°C. Spread the pumpkin seeds out on a baking tray and cook them for about 10 minutes, until they turn a very light gold and smell nutty.

While the pumpkin seeds are cooking, heat the grill to high. Line the grill pan with foil and arrange the tomatoes cut side up on it, season, and grill about 5 cm/2 in from the heat until they start to blacken along the edges, 10 to 15 minutes.

Place the pumpkin seeds, tomatoes, garlic, onions, olive oil, about 1 tbsp of fresh lemon juice, chipotle chilli sauce and some seasoning in a food processor and process until you have a coarse paste. Taste and adjust the seasoning, and add a bit more lemon juice and chipotle chilli sauce if the flavour is not bright or spicy enough – it needs to have quite a bite. Add the 15 g/½ oz of coriander and process again, just until it is coarsely chopped and the sauce is flecked with green. The sauce can be prepared up to this point a day in advance and refrigerated; bring back to room temperature before serving.

Transfer the sauce to a large bowl and fold in the butter beans and cherry tomatoes. Check the seasoning.

Sprinkle with the coriander leaves and serve immediately.

FRIED EGGS YUCATÁN-STYLE
Huevos Motuleños

This dish is a speciality of the southern state of Yucatán, renowned for its Mayan ruins and its glorious Caribbean coast, although the best version we ate was in San Cristóbal de las Casas, a village in neighbouring, mountainous, jungle-covered Chiapas. The overnight bus from Oaxaca stopped in Tuxtla Gutiérrez, the dreary capital of the state, just before dawn and we all clambered out, stiff and bleary-eyed, to find some breakfast. Fifteen minutes later, well provisioned with fresh fruit, juice and *tortas* of spicy scrambled eggs to sustain us during the last leg of the journey, we started climbing steeply through the swirling morning mists towards San Cristóbal, way up in the Chiapas highlands. It was a two hour drive, one hairpin bend after the other, and the scenery took our breath away: the violet sky lightened rapidly and then turned a soft shell pink as the sun rose behind the mountain peaks. Looking down towards Tuxtla, we found that it had disappeared beneath an eiderdown of vapour, and we were floating in a strange, limitless world of rippling mountains and pastel-coloured strips of cloud drifting through the air all around us. We arrived in San Cristóbal in time for a second breakfast at the lovely Casa Na Bolom, an old colonial house with a bougainvillea-filled central courtyard. It was the home of Swiss anthropologist, Trudi Blom, who made a special study of the *Lacandones*, the direct descendants of the Mayas. I stayed at Na Bolom in my late teens, before going off with Trudi into the jungle for a week-long trek on mule-back to see the *Lacandones* in their natural habitat. The house is now a museum as well as a hotel, and I was thrilled to find photographs of the *Lacandones* I had met so many years ago on the walls. We saw modern-day *Lacandones* at the Palenque ruins, but the sight of them was not quite so magical, their traditional costume and bows and arrows rather at variance with their gaudy wristwatches...

We had these *huevos motuleños* at Na Bolom that morning, and they were incredibly comforting and energising after our long bus trip.

Serves 2

1 x quantity Refried Beans (page 16)
4 rashers streaky bacon or pancetta, rinded

150 ml/¼ pint vegetable oil
1 large ripe plantain, about 250 g/9 oz, peeled and sliced into 1 cm/ ½ in rounds
4 eggs
150 ml/¼ pint soured cream or Greek-style plain yoghurt
100 g/4 oz Farmhouse Cheddar cheese, coarsely grated
15 g/½ oz fresh coriander, coarsely chopped
Sea salt and freshly ground black pepper

Heat the refried beans in a frying pan over gentle heat.

Line a large baking tray with a double thickness of kitchen paper and turn the oven on to its lowest setting. Grill or fry the bacon or pancetta until crisp, place on the baking tray and keep warm in the oven.

While the bacon is cooking, heat the vegetable oil in a non-stick frying pan and add the plantain, browning it quickly on both sides – keep it moving around in the oil as it sticks easily. With a slotted spoon, transfer it to the baking tray in the oven.

Break the eggs into the oil in the frying pan and fry them sunny side-up.

Season, place on two warm plates, drizzle with soured cream or yoghurt and sprinkle with cheese and coriander.

Serve immediately with the refried beans, plantain and bacon.

El Chacmool

BLACK BEAN AND PRAWN *CHILAQUILES*
Chilaquiles Negros con Camarones

Chilaquiles are almost an institution in Mexico, drawn from poverty cooking: a handful of stale tortillas moistened with a bit of tomato sauce. They are served mainly at breakfast, and they are delicious in all their forms, from the simplest and most basic, like *Enjitomatadas* (page 82) and *Enfrijoladas* (page 20), to a sophisticated dish like this one which we came across in Zihuatanejo on the Pacific coast. The waitress at the beautiful Villa del Sol Hotel proudly informed us that *El Chef Ejecutivo*, the Head Chef, had trained in London, Paris and New York, and his food is certainly *alta cocina mexicana*, Mexican haute cuisine, perfectly suited to his well-heeled, international clientèle.

Serves 4

60 ml/4 tbsp olive oil
250 g/9 oz red onions, peeled and sliced
1 red chilli, deseeded and sliced
1 x quantity Basic Beans, made with black beans (page 11)
1 tbsp chipotle chilli sauce (see Resources)
250 g/9 oz plain tortilla chips
200 g/7 oz raw king prawns, shelled and deveined
15 g/½ oz fresh coriander, coarsely chopped
250 ml/8 fl oz soured cream or Greek-style plain yoghurt
100 g/4 oz Feta cheese
Sea salt and freshly ground black pepper

Heat the olive oil in a frying pan and add the red onions and chilli. Cook gently, stirring occasionally, for about 15 minutes, until they are wilted and just starting to brown.

While the onions are cooking, drain the beans, reserving the cooking liquid and discarding the bay leaf. Place them in a large, deep frying pan or wok and heat them gently, mashing them with a potato masher to a coarse purée. Stir in the chipotle chilli sauce and just enough of the cooking liquid to bring the beans to a soupy consistency. Add the tortilla chips and turn them over and over in the bean purée with a large spoon until they are well coated and starting to soften. Keep them warm while you cook the prawns.

When the onions are ready, add the prawns and stir-fry for a few minutes, until they just turn pink. Season and fold in the coriander.

Spoon the prawns over the chilaquiles, drizzle with about half the soured cream or yoghurt, crumble over the Feta cheese and serve immediately, straight from the wok, with extra cream or yoghurt on the side

SCALLOPS WITH REFRIED BEANS
Callos de Hacha con Frijoles Refritos

The seafood in Veracruz on the Gulf of Mexico is quite outstanding and fresh beyond belief – you can see it being unloaded from the fishing boats in the morning and know that it will be dished up in the restaurants that very lunch-time. The best place to eat it is in the market, where you can sit at a counter and watch it being cooked with a minimum of fuss and facilities, and served with plenty of flair and panache. The sweetness of the scallops works wonderfully with the earthy beans and the smoky, spicy *salsa*.

Serves 4

½ tbsp chipotle chilli sauce (see Resources)
1 x quantity Raw Tomato Salsa without chillies (page 201)
30 ml/2 tbsp olive oil
12 large scallops, cleaned and muscle removed
1 x quantity Refried Beans (page 16), heated
15 g/½ oz flat leaf parsley, coarsely chopped
Sea salt and freshly ground black pepper

Stir the chipotle chilli sauce into the salsa.

Heat the olive oil in a heavy frying pan. Season the scallops lightly and fry them on high heat for 2 to 3 minutes on each side, just long enough to create a light golden crust; scallops need to be barely cooked, until just warm in the middle – any more than that and they will be tough, rubbery and tasteless.

Divide the refried beans between four plates, top with the scallops and sprinkle with parsley. Spoon the salsa around the beans and serve immediately.

PRAWN TACOS
Tacos de Camarón

Patricia Quintana is the national *grande dame* of Mexican cuisine. Ixote, her lovely restaurant on Presidente Mazaryk in Mexico City, specialises in pre-Hispanic food and adds a touch of sophistication to traditional recipes – a true contrast to the contemporary ultra-modern interior of glass and mirrors softened with abstract ethnic motifs in warm earth colours. She makes these tacos from Baja California with lobster, and they are truly wonderful, the sweetness of the seafood a perfect partner for the creamy soft beans and the vibrant *salsa*. However, prawns are a good, easy and considerably cheaper substitute, even if not quite as luxurious. And although she serves her lobster tacos with typically northern flour tortillas, I much prefer the flavour of the corn ones in this case.

Serves 2

75 g/3 oz pinto beans
2 tbsp/30 ml olive oil
175 g/6 oz red onions, peeled and finely sliced
200 g/7 oz raw king prawns, shelled and deveined
½ x quantity Raw Tomato Salsa (page 201)
6 corn tortillas, warmed

Rinse the beans in a colander under cold, running water. Put them in a small saucepan, add enough water to cover them by 5 cm/2 in, and simmer, covered, until totally soft, about 2 hours. Check them every now and then to make sure they have at least 1 cm/½ in of water over them. Drain well, return to the saucepan, stir in 1 tbsp of olive oil and some seasoning, and keep warm – or reheat just before serving. The beans can be prepared several days ahead and refrigerated.

Heat the remaining olive oil in a medium frying pan, add the onions and some seasoning, and cook over medium to high heat, stirring often, until they just start to soften but still have a bit of crunch to them, about 10 minutes. Add the prawns and stir-fry until they turn firm and pink. Check the seasoning and transfer to a warm serving dish.

To serve, place the beans in a small warm serving dish and arrange on the table with the prawns, tortillas and salsa. Make the tacos by placing a spoonful of prawns on a warm tortilla, add some beans and salsa, roll up and eat immediately.

GRILLED SALMON WITH BLACK BEAN SAUCE
Salmón en Salsa Negra

The colour scheme in this dish is almost too dramatic! We had a similar combination in Tulúm, on the Caribbean coast – a whole roasted red snapper sat on a bed of refried beans, with a garnish of red pickled onions, soured cream and sliced radishes, and a choice of *salsas*. It looked spectacular and tasted delicious but I find that the richness of salmon is an even better foil to the spicy, savoury beans, although this does make it more *nouvelle cuisine* than authentic Mexican!

Serves 4

60 ml/4 tbsp olive oil
125 g/4 ½ oz red onions, peeled and coarsely chopped
2 garlic cloves, peeled and chopped
1 red chilli, deseeded and chopped
75 g/3 oz pancetta or smoked bacon, rinded and coarsely chopped
1 tsp cumin seeds, ground medium fine in a mortar or spice grinder
½ x quantity Basic Beans, made with black beans (page 11)
4 x skinless salmon fillets, about 175 g/6 oz each
250 ml/8 fl oz soured cream or Greek-style plain yoghurt
15 g/½ oz fresh coriander, coarsely chopped
1 x quantity Raw Tomato Salsa (page 201)
Sea salt and freshly ground black pepper

Heat 1 tbsp of olive oil in a medium-sized saucepan and add the onions, garlic, chilli and pancetta or bacon. Cook over medium heat for about 10 minutes, until soft and just starting to brown. Add the cumin and cook for a further 3 minutes. Remove the bay leaf from the beans and pour them with their cooking liquid into the onion mixture. Add some seasoning, bring to the boil and simmer for 10 minutes. Cool slightly before transferring to a food processor and processing until fairly smooth. Check the seasoning and reheat gently.

When the sauce is ready, heat the grill to high. Line the grill pan with foil, arrange the salmon fillets on it, brush them with 1 tbsp of olive oil and sprinkle with salt and pepper. Grill about 3 cm / 1 ¼ in from the heat for 5 minutes, without turning them over, until they are just firm to the touch with a bit of bounce left in them.

While the fish is cooking, mix the soured cream or yoghurt with the remaining olive oil and some salt.

Divide the black bean purée between four warm plates, top with the salmon, drizzle with soured cream or yoghurt and sprinkle with fresh coriander.

Serve immediately, with the salsa on the side.

Salmón en salsa negra

CASSEROLE OF PORK WITH FRUIT AND LENTILS
Tinga de Cerdo con Fruta y Lentejas

Mulato chillies are a shy star in this dish – black and wizened, with a distinct whiff of licorice and prunes. Low on the heat scale, they add a glow rather than fire, as well as bitter sweetness. This is a distinctly post-Conquest dish, since pork, lentils and grapes followed the Spaniards to the New World, as did the Moorish predilection for combining meat with fruit. Nevertheless, it sits well on the Mexican table, the chillies giving it sparkle and a discreet contrast to the sweetness of the tropical fruit. The simplicity of plain boiled rice matches the stew to perfection and soaks up its rich, hot, sweet sauce. The casserole keeps well for several days in the refrigerator, and if anything, the flavour benefits from being allowed to mature.

Serves 4

50 g/2 oz mulato chillies (see Resources)
1 large plantain, about 250 g/9 oz, peeled and sliced into 1 cm/½ in rounds
60 ml/4 tbsp olive oil
750 g/1 ¾ lb tomatoes, halved
500 g/18 oz stewing pork, cubed
125 g/4 ½ oz pancetta or smoked bacon, rinded and coarsely chopped
200 g/7 oz onions, peeled and coarsely chopped
2 garlic cloves, peeled and crushed
125 g/4 ½ oz green lentils, rinsed under cold running water
25 g/1 oz raisins
750 ml/1 ¼ pints water
½ small pineapple, about 375 g/13 oz with skin, peeled and cubed
15 g/½ oz mint, coarsely chopped
Sea salt and freshly ground black pepper
Cooked rice, to serve

Heat a heavy frying pan over medium heat and toast the chillies, pressing down on them with a spatula, until they start to smell aromatic, about 3 minutes. Flip them over and do the same on the other side. Place them in a bowl, cover with boiling water, put a small saucepan lid or plate on top to keep them submerged, and leave to soak for 30 minutes. Drain them, remove the stalks, seeds and ribs, and set aside.

Heat the grill to high. Line the grill pan with foil, place the plantain slices on it, brush them with 1 tbsp of olive oil, and grill 5 cm/2 in from the heat for about 3 minutes on each side, until soft and lightly browned. Lift the foil and plantain out of the pan and set aside, leaving the grill on.

Line the grill pan again with foil and arrange the tomatoes cut side up on it. Grill 5 cm/2 in from the heat for about 15 minutes, until softened and slightly charred. Place in a food processor, add the chillies and process until smooth.

While the plantain and tomatoes are grilling, heat 2 tbsp of olive oil in a heavy frying pan and add the pork and bacon. Cook over medium heat, stirring often, until well browned, about 15 minutes. Remove to a plate, add another tablespoon of oil to the frying pan and cook the onions and garlic until soft and golden. Add the tomato purée and stir-fry for a few minutes to thicken. Return the pork and bacon to the pan, add the lentils, raisins, water and some pepper, bring to the boil and simmer for 25 minutes, stirring occasionally. Add the pineapple and cook for a further 20 minutes. If it looks rather dry, add a bit more water.

When the pork has finished cooking, stir in the plantain slices. Check the seasoning and add some salt if necessary – the bacon may have made it salty enough.

Sprinkle with mint and serve immediately.

STEW
Puchero

Pucheros are found all over Latin America and recipes abound, each one with its own national quirk or local twist. The seasonings will vary depending on the country and the area, with chillies and spices used according to whim or tradition. However, there is no doubt as to *puchero*'s European origins, as it almost invariably contains pork in one form or another – and although it usually features a combination of different meats for special occasions, an everyday *puchero* like this one is simpler and served in most provincial restaurants as part of the set menu, the *comida corrida*. Piggy bits aside, the raisins in particular point to its Old World antecedents and Moorish tendencies, as do the chickpeas, which also landed in America with the Spanish *Conquistadores* – but the *ancho* chillies, with their fruity richness and warmth, place the dish firmly in the New World. *Pucheros* are hearty, rustic food, singing with flavour and deeply comforting; the rice with plantains on page 250 is the perfect accompaniment. The *puchero* can be refrigerated for several days, and like all stews, actually improves with keeping.

Serves 4

50 g/2 oz ancho chillies (see Resources)
750 g/1 ¾ lb tomatoes, halved
1 tbsp olive oil
4 meaty pork belly chops, about 1 kg/2 ¼ lb
275 g/10 oz red onions, peeled and sliced
3 garlic cloves, peeled and crushed
100 g/4 oz chorizo sausage, cut into 1 cm/½ in rounds
1 large red pepper, about 175 g/6 oz, cut into 1 cm/½ in wide strips
1 large yellow pepper, about 175 g/6 oz, cut into 1 cm/½ in wide strips
1 heaped tsp dried Mexican oregano (see Resources)
30 g/1 ¼ oz raisins
450 g/1 lb sweet potato, peeled and cut into 2 cm/1 in pieces
1 x 400 g/14 oz tin chickpeas, rinsed and drained
250 ml/8 fl oz water
15 g/½ oz slivered toasted almonds

15 g/½ oz flat leaf parsley, coarsely chopped
Sea salt and freshly ground black pepper
Plain Rice with Plantains, to serve (page 250)

Tear the chillies open and remove the stems and seeds. Heat a heavy, dry frying pan over medium heat, lay the chillies out flat on it and toast them for 2 to 3 minutes on each side, pressing down on them with a spatula, just until they smell aromatic. Remove them to a bowl, pour boiling water over them, place a small saucepan lid or plate on top to keep them submerged, and leave to soak for 30 minutes. Drain and set aside.

Heat the grill to high. Line the grill pan with foil, arrange the tomatoes cut side up on it and grill about 5 cm/2 in from the heat, until soft and starting to blacken around the edges, about 20 minutes. Cool slightly and purée with the chillies in a food processor until fairly smooth.

Heat the olive oil in a heavy casserole and brown the chops well on all sides – be sure to get some colour on them as this is essential to the flavour of the finished dish. Remove the chops to a plate and add the onions, garlic, chorizo and peppers to the frying pan. Cook over medium heat, stirring occasionally, until they soften and start to brown, about 15 minutes. Sprinkle in the oregano and some seasoning, and cook for a further 3 minutes. Stir in the tomato and chilli purée, raisins, sweet potato, chickpeas and water, then nestle the chops down into the sauce, making sure they are well covered with liquid.

Heat the oven to 180°C/350°F/gas 4/fan oven 160°C. Cover the casserole with a lid or a double thickness of foil, and bake in the oven for one hour. Remove from the oven, give everything a good stir and check the seasoning.

Sprinkle with almonds and parsley and serve immediately with the rice.

Itzcuintli

sun

Tonatiuh

Tonatiuh, Aztec god of the Sun, was the primary source of life on Earth. Every day, as he repeated his passage across the heavens, he brought warmth and light to the land and the crops and thereby food to feed the hungry people. Corn was, and still is, a chief staple of the Mexican diet, and while it was guarded by Xochipilli, the corn deity, it looked to Tonatiuh to ripen it until it was bright gold in the image of the Sun itself. It must be said, however, that Tonatiuh was a bringer of death as well as life: he was god of women who died in childbirth, and also god of warriors, and prisoners of battle were regularly sacrificed to him. This darkness is reflected perhaps in the colour of the corn of the central Mexican plateau: inky blue and purple, like the night sky.

Tortillas are the 'bread' of Mexico and virtually no meal is complete without them. There was no wheat until the arrival of the Spaniards, and although bread is eaten at breakfast and tortillas made of wheat are eaten in the North, corn tortillas are the quintessential Mexican food. Fresh and warm from the griddle, they are intoxicatingly fragrant and gratifying.

The basic corn dough, the *masa*, has been made for centuries by soaking and boiling the dried corn kernels with lime and then grinding them while still damp. This was originally done by hand on a lava rock *metate* and a ball of *masa* was then patted out into a disc between two hands. Nowadays, the *masa* is ground in electric mills and tortillas are made mechanically – few Mexican housewives make their own, except in very rural areas.

When I was small, our cook still made our tortillas at home, and the sound of her patting them out is one of my earliest childhood memories. Her hands would move at tremendous speed, reminding me of a fluttering butterfly. She would then flip them on to a hot earthenware griddle, a *comal*, cook them briefly on both sides, and send them to the table in a special tortilla 'cosy' to keep them warm. We would butter them, sprinkle them with salt, then roll them up and bend them into a U shape to stop the melted butter from dribbling out. As I grew older, machine-made tortillas took over but they were still freshly made every morning and sold by *tortilleras* from door to door in the wealthier residential areas of Mexico City. I remember ours so well: a squat elderly woman with two long grey plaits and a big straw hat. Her basket of tortillas sat on a wooden trolley, just a couple of planks with four little wheels. She never needed to ring the doorbell: all the housemaids could hear her quite clearly as she walked along the street, pulling her rattling trolley behind her, and they would be waiting for her at the front door of every house, the housekeeping purse in their hands.

Although there is a knack to them and they take practice, tortillas are not difficult to make in a manual tortilla press and it is well worth the effort just to experience the fragrance and comfort of a freshly made tortilla. I have to admit, however, that I use bought tortillas or tortilla chips most of the time. Ordinary supermarket tortillas, such as Old El Paso, are far from the real thing but they work fairly well in dishes like tortilla casseroles, *enchiladas* or *quesadillas*. The Discovery brand is superior, but a more authentic and better flavoured and textured tortilla is available from Cool Chile Company (see Resources), who make their own tortillas (which freeze well). They also supply dried *masa* and presses if you want to have a go at making tortillas yourself. I use their *masa* for *tamales, sopes* and all the other glorious *antojitos* made from corn.

CHILLIED SWEETCORN
Elote Enchilado

Corn on the cob is sold on every street corner in Mexico, piping hot and brushed with any number of flavoured butters, seasoned oils and chilli powders. Wending our way in and out of the street stalls and around the balloon sellers along Calle 2 Norte in Puebla one evening after a heavy downpour, we realised that we were the only ones not munching on a savoury, spicy corn cob. We stopped at the next *marchanta* sitting on a small stool in front of a large two-handled metal container full of steaming corn. She had cooked it at home just half an hour ago, she explained to us, and her son had helped her to carry it to her special patch on 2 Norte. The cobs would keep hot for a good couple of hours as the container provided excellent insulation. She fished two of them out with a pair of tongs, stuck small wooden skewers in each end, brushed them with brick-red butter, and then rolled them deftly in a plate of grated cheese. It was not easy to eat as we continued our evening *paseo* back to the central *zócalo*, and we ended up with chilli butter and cheese all over our faces, but it was delicious beyond words.

2 corn on the cob
50 g/2 oz butter
1 tsp chilli powder, or to taste
50 g/2 oz grated Parmesan cheese
4 cocktail sticks or small skewers

Steam or boil the corn until tender – the time will depend on the age and size of the corn, but reckon on about 20 minutes.

While the corn is cooking, melt the butter in a frying pan large enough to hold the corn. Stir in the chilli powder. Spread the cheese out in a roasting tray or large plate.

When the corn is cooked, drain it well and insert the cocktail sticks or skewers at each end. Transfer to the frying pan and roll the corn around in the spicy butter, coating it generously. Now repeat the process with the cheese, rolling the corn in it until it has a thick coating. Place the corn on two warm plates, drizzle with any remaining butter, and sprinkle with any remaining cheese.

Serve immediately with plenty of paper napkins, because this is messy food!

SCRAMBLED EGGS WITH TORTILLA CHIPS
Migas

The perfect breakfast or brunch dish, served all over Mexico with cups of steaming coffee and a basket of sweet breads. One of its greatest delights is the contrast in texture between the chewy tortilla bits and the soft creamy eggs, and it is well worth doubling the recipe because left-overs make a delicious, moist filling for a *torta*, a bread roll, to be enjoyed for lunch the following day, ideally while sitting on a bench in the warm sunshine. Mexicans do not add milk or cream to their scrambled eggs, so the curds are never as soft and smooth as I am used to, but the tomatoes they are cooked with in this case produce a lovely, velvety texture.

Serves 2

30 ml/2 tbsp olive oil
2 garlic cloves, peeled and crushed
1 mild green or red chilli, deseeded and finely sliced
1 tsp cumin seeds, coarsely ground in a mortar or spice grinder
200 g/7 oz tomatoes, coarsely chopped
25 g/1 oz butter
4 eggs, beaten
65 g/2 ½ oz plain tortilla chips
1 fat spring onion, finely sliced
15 g/½ oz fresh coriander, coarsely chopped
Sea salt and freshly ground black pepper

Heat the olive oil in a small frying pan and fry the garlic and chilli for 5 minutes, until just softened. Add the cumin and cook, stirring, for 1 minute, then add the tomatoes. Cook for a further 10 minutes, stirring occasionally, to thicken the mixture. Season and set aside.

Melt the butter in a pan and pour in the eggs. Season and cook over low heat, stirring constantly, until the eggs just start to set. Add the tomato sauce and tortilla chips and stir them gently into the eggs, pushing down slightly on the chips to break them up a bit. Continue to cook until the mixture is softly scrambled.

Check the seasoning, sprinkle with spring onion and coriander, and serve immediately.

Pán dulce

COUNTRY EGGS
Huevos Rancheros

A traditional breakfast dish and a marvellous way to kick-start both your palate and your day! Fried eggs, crisp tortillas, spicy tomato sauce, sometimes a sprinkling of cheese or some sliced avocado. I find the frying of tortillas as well as eggs a bit of a palaver and therefore tend to use *enjitomatadas* (page 82), which rolls the tortilla and sauce part of the dish into one. The eggs are delicious with refried beans – one of my favourite suppers which effortlessly transports me across the world, I don't even have to close my eyes, the flavours and aromas do it all.

Serves 2

1 x quantity Tomatoed Tortillas (page 82), without cheese
60 ml/4 tbsp vegetable oil
4 eggs
30 g/1 ¼ oz Parmesan cheese, freshly grated
15 g/½ oz fresh coriander, coarsely chopped
Sea salt and freshly ground black pepper

When the sauce for the Tomatoed Tortillas is nearing the end of its simmering time, heat the oil in a large frying pan and fry the eggs sunny side up.

While they are cooking, add the tortilla chips to the tomato sauce and turn them over and over with a large spoon until they are well coated.

Divide the Tomatoed Tortillas between two warm plates, slide the eggs on top, and sprinkle with cheese, coriander and some seasoning.

Serve immediately.

SAVOURY *TAMALES*
Tamales de Picadillo

The *tamal* vendor would blow his steam whistle as he pushed his small barrel-shaped trolley along the street. It must have had hot coals in the bottom, because his *tamales* were always piping hot – light, fragrant and incredibly delicious, well worth spending my pocket money on. They came in just three flavours: red chilli, green chilli and sweet. The green ones took the roof off my mouth, the red ones were deeply savoury with a bearable amount of heat; but the sweet ones were my favourites: studded with raisins and nuts, heady with cinnamon and cloves, perfect for breakfast.

Tamales are among the oldest and most authentic of Mexican dishes, served to the conquering Spaniards in Moctezuma's splendid banqueting hall. A simple cornmeal dough enclosing a filling is wrapped in either corn husks or banana leaves, depending on the region, and then steamed, allowing the flavour and aroma of the filling – and the envelope – to permeate the dough. Nowadays lard is traditionally added to the *masa*, giving it a light, almost cakey texture – I tend to use butter as neither my heart nor I are frightfully keen on the taste or effects of lard. A *salsa* or cooked sauce is often served with *tamales,* but they are lovely on their own. The wrapping part is a bit fiddly and time-consuming, so keep this recipe for a rainy day when you are happy to spend relaxed, creative time in the kitchen. The results are well worth it.

Makes 8 tamales

100 g/4 oz cornhusks (see Resources)
75 g/3 oz butter, softened
½ tsp salt
½ tsp baking powder
1 tsp bouillon powder
250 g/9 oz masa harina (see Resources)
400 ml/14 fl oz warm water
½ x quantity Picadillo (page 235)
String (optional)

Put the cornhusks in a large bowl and pour a kettle of boiling water over them. Place a small saucepan lid or plate on top of them to keep them submerged and leave them to soften and soak for a couple of hours or even overnight.

Process the butter, salt, baking and bouillon powders in a food processor until creamy and well blended. Add about a quarter of the masa harina followed by a quarter of the water, processing in between and repeating the procedure with the remaining masa harina and water until you have a thick batter.

Drain the cornhusks, lay them out on a dishcloth, cover them with a second dishcloth, and pat them dry. Arrange enough of them on the work surface to make a square about 15cm/6 in x 15cm/6 in, overlapping several pieces of husk if necessary. Spread ⅛ of the batter on the square, leaving a 2 cm/¾ in border. Spoon ⅛ of the Picadillo in the centre of the batter. Fold one side of the cornhusks up and over the batter and the filling, enclosing it all completely, then fold up the other side in the same way, to make a parcel. Don't worry if it is not particularly tidy, that is what tamales look like! Carefully pick the parcel up and set it aside, seam side down. Repeat with the rest of the batter and filling.

When the tamales are all made, they can either be steamed as they are, seam side down, or you can tie them up like a present, which makes them slightly easier to handle once they are cooked and improves the presentation. In Mexico, strips of cornhusk or banana leaf are used, which looks very ethnic and natural – but this also adds to the fiddliness of making tamales, so I use string!

Line a steamer with corn husks or baking parchment and put it in a large saucepan with 3 cm/1 ¼ in of boiling water. Arrange the parcels in the steamer, cover the pan and steam the tamales for 1 hour and 30 minutes.

To serve, place one or two tamales on each plate and provide a pair of scissors to cut the string.

Any leftover cornhusks can be left to dry out completely and used on another occasion.

Tamales

LIME SOUP
Sopa de Lima

This lovely soup is a speciality of the southern province of Yucatán and seems to feature on every restaurant menu. Although it is served hot, it is surprisingly refreshing and full of bright, zappy flavours, which can on occasions be too mouth-puckering for my taste – the native bitter oranges (*naranjas agrias*) are traditionally used and are very sour indeed. The fiery *habañero* chilli is also traditional – so be sure to remove it before serving to lessen its wrath. We ate this colourful version, with its bits of citrus, at the museum restaurant adjacent to the Mayan ruins of Uxmal – the menu was predictably touristy and unappealing, but the soup was a winner and re-energised us instantly. If blood oranges are available, do use them as their vivid colour and faint flavour of blackberries take the soup to new heights. Leftover chicken from the Sunday roast is perfect for this recipe.

Serves 4

45 ml/3 tbsp olive oil
500 g/18 oz onions, peeled and coarsely chopped
10 garlic cloves, peeled and crushed
1 tsp cumin seeds, coarsely ground in a mortar or spice grinder
500 g/18 oz tomatoes, skinned and coarsely chopped
1 habañero chilli, fresh or dried (see Resources)
2 pink grapefruit
2 large navel oranges
1 litre/1 ¾ pints chicken or vegetable stock, or water mixed with 1 tbsp bouillon powder
250 g/9 oz cooked chicken, shredded
1 lime, juiced
15 g/½ oz fresh coriander, coarsely chopped
125 g/4 ½ oz plain tortilla chips
Sea salt and freshly ground black pepper

Heat the olive oil in a medium saucepan and add the onions and garlic. Cook gently, stirring occasionally, until soft and deep gold, about 30 minutes. Sprinkle in the cumin and cook for a further 3 minutes, then add the tomatoes, chilli and some seasoning. Raise the heat to medium and leave it to cook for about 15 minutes, until the tomatoes have released most of their moisture and the mixture has thickened.

While the vegetables are cooking, finely grate the rind from one grapefruit and one orange into a small bowl, then squeeze the juice from the fruit and add it to the rind. Peel the remaining grapefruit and orange, slice out the segments with a sharp knife, dice them and place in a cup. Squeeze the juice from the membranes into the small bowl with the rind and juice.

Add the stock to the tomatoes and onions, bring to the boil and simmer for 10 minutes. Fish out and discard the habañero chilli – or leave it in if you dare! Stir in the fruit rind and juice, then the chicken and bring the soup back to the boil. Check the seasoning and add half the lime juice; taste the soup to see if it is sharp enough – if the oranges were very sweet, you may need to add the whole quantity of lime juice.

Ladle into warm soup bowls and serve immediately garnished with the diced citrus segments, coriander and a handful of tortilla chips.

POBLANO CHILLI SOUP

Sopa de Poblano

The rich, velvety smoothness of this traditional, softly coloured soup is the first impression it will make on you. The second or third spoonful will bring the gentle, smoky warmth of the chilli. Then you will notice the sweetness and crunch of the corn. By the time you have finished the bowl, you will be feeling deliciously soothed yet energised, relaxed but ready for anything. The overall effect is incomprehensibly therapeutic – unless of course the cook has been a bit heavy-handed with the chilli, but that is unusual as the *poblano's* heat is very temperate and its dried relative, the *chipotle*, is easily controlled. If *poblanos* are not available, green peppers will work perfectly and will simply need a bit of bolstering from extra chipotle chilli sauce.

Serves 2 generously

500 g/18 oz poblano chillies (see Resources) or green peppers
1 tbsp olive oil
175 g/6 oz onions, peeled and coarsely chopped
500 ml/17 fl oz chicken or vegetable stock, or water mixed with 1 tsp bouillon powder
150 ml/¼ pint double cream
1 tsp chipotle chilli sauce or to taste (see Resources)
100 g/4 oz tinned or frozen sweetcorn, defrosted and well drained
Soured cream or Greek-style plain yoghurt
Sea salt and freshly ground black pepper

Heat the grill to high. Line the grill pan with foil and place the chillies or peppers on it. Grill them 10 cm/4 in from the heat, turning them as needed, until they are soft and slightly blackened all over. Set aside to cool, then peel, discard the stem, core and seeds, and chop the flesh very coarsely.

While the chillies are grilling, heat the oil in a medium saucepan and add the onions and some seasoning. Cook gently, stirring occasionally, until lightly golden, about 20 minutes. Pour in the stock, add the cooked chillies, bring to the boil and simmer for 30 minutes. Cool slightly before blending in a food processor or blender until totally smooth. Return to the saucepan, stir in the cream, chipotle chilli sauce and sweetcorn, and bring back to the boil. Taste for seasoning and heat – it should just have a bit of smoky bite.

Ladle into 2 warm soup bowls, add a good spoonful of soured cream or yoghurt and serve immediately.

SWEETCORN SOUP WITH AVOCADO *SALSA*
Sopa de Elote con Salsa de Aguacate

The rich sweetness of the corn is a wonderful foil for the lively, sharp *salsa*, and the colour scheme is glorious! The soup can be served hot or cold, although I much prefer it hot, even on a blistering day. Corn tortillas are the obvious accompaniment, but *totopos*, tortilla chips, are more fun and the thickness of the soup makes it easy to scoop up a bit of soup and a bit of *salsa* at the same time; this method does not save much on the washing up but it will certainly make you laugh.

Serves 4

30 ml/2 tbsp olive oil
200 g/7 oz onions, peeled and coarsely chopped
400 g/14 oz tinned or frozen sweetcorn, defrosted and well drained
750 ml/1 ¼ pints milk
1 bay leaf
Sea salt and freshly ground black pepper

1 x quantity Avocado Salsa (page 163)

Heat the olive oil in a medium saucepan, add the onions and cook for about 10 minutes, stirring occasionally, until softened but not brown. Stir in the sweetcorn and some seasoning, then the milk and the bay leaf. Bring to the boil, cover the pan and simmer very gently, stirring occasionally, for 30 minutes. Cool slightly and process in a food processor until very smooth. Strain the soup through the medium blade of a mouli-légumes or a wide mesh sieve – do not be tempted to skip this step as one of the charms of the soup is its velvety smoothness. Check the seasoning.

Ladle the soup into four warm bowls, place a good spoonful of salsa in the middle, and serve immediately with the rest of the salsa on the side to add as you eat the soup.

If you are serving the soup cold, allow it to cool completely and refrigerate until totally cold. The soup can be prepared up to 48 hours ahead of time.

Diseño Purépecha

TOSTADAS

Tostadas are a sort of Mexican open sandwich – a crisp, crunchy tortilla topped with a variety of ingredients. Large supermarkets stock curved tostada "shells", but they do not work for this recipe – a flat *tostada* is what you need and for some reason they are not as readily available. However, it is easy to fry tortillas briefly in some olive oil and the texture is infinitely superior. A traditional *tostada* like this one is an *antojito*, a snack rather than a meal, but if you are looking for something more substantial and protein-rich, try replacing the refried beans with stir-fried king prawns or the *Picadillo* on page 235. I have also had it with smoked tuna or swordfish on the Pacific coast, which is delicious if almost too sophisticated for such a conventional dish. A *tostada* is perfect finger food but needs to be eaten without undue delay – hold the edges with your thumb and index finger, and use your remaining fingers to support the underside, thus preventing the whole *tostada* from collapsing suddenly and totally unexpectedly and ending up as a soggy mess in your lap! This used to happen to me often, as the weight and moisture of the topping took their toll while I was busy chatting.

Serves 6

45 ml/3 tbsp olive oil
6 corn tortillas
1 x quantity Refried Beans (page 16), heated
300 g/11 oz cherry tomatoes, quartered
6 Cos lettuce leaves, finely sliced
1 large ripe avocado, peeled and diced
150 g/5 oz mild goat's cheese
250 ml/8 fl oz soured cream or Greek-style plain yoghurt

Heat the olive oil in a large frying pan over medium heat and fry the tortillas for a couple of minutes on each side, until golden. Remove to a baking tray lined with kitchen paper to drain. When they are cool, spread each one with some warm refried beans, then sprinkle with tomatoes, shredded lettuce, avocado and crumbled goat's cheese, and finally drizzle with soured cream or yoghurt.

Serve immediately before the tostadas go soft and the beans get cold.

MASA TARTLETS WITH PLANTAIN
Sopes de Plátano Macho

Watching Mexican cooks shaping *sopes* in the market *fondas* is mesmerising: they work incredibly fast, shaping them while they cook, seemingly impervious to the heat of the pan, and the end result is a perfectly shaped tartlet case. My attempts at making *sopes* have been more successful some times than others as much depends on getting exactly the right amount of water into the dough – and *masa harina* seems to absorb more water one day than the next... However, with a relatively solid topping, as in this recipe, it does not actually matter if the tartlet sides are not high or even enough. Although lard is traditionally used, I have found that butter gives a lighter, pleasantly cakey texture and a better flavour. Needless to say, Mexican cooks do not use wholemeal flour, but I like its slight grittiness.

Makes 4 sopes

For the sopes:-
125 g/4 ½ oz masa harina (see Resources)
30 g/1 ¼ oz wholemeal flour
15 g/½ oz butter, softened
½ tsp salt
½ tsp baking powder
175 ml/6 fl oz warm water
30 ml/2 tbsp olive oil

For the topping:-
1 large ripe plantain, about 250 g/9 oz, peeled and sliced into 1 cm/½ in thick rounds
1 tbsp olive oil
175 g/6 oz smoked streaky bacon rashers, rinded
½ x recipe Refried Beans (page 16), heated
100 g/4 oz Farmhouse Cheddar cheese, coarsely grated
200 ml/7 fl oz soured cream or Greek-style plain yoghurt

Place the masa harina, flour, butter, salt and baking powder in a food processor and process briefly. With the motor running, pour in the water and process until it is just amalgamated. Scrape into a bowl, knead into a ball, cover with clingfilm and set aside to rest for 30 minutes.

Heat the grill to high. Line the grill pan with foil and arrange the plantain slices on it. Brush them with the olive oil and grill them 5 cm/2 in from the heat for about 5 minutes on each side, until lightly browned. Transfer them with a spatula to a plate lined with kitchen paper to drain. Arrange the bacon on the grill pan and grill it until crisp. Cool, then crumble over the plantains.

Heat the oven to its lowest setting and put the plantain and bacon to warm while you make the sopes. Warm a serving dish as well.

Divide the dough into 4 balls and flatten them into circles about ¾ cm/1/3 in thick. Heat a heavy, preferably non-stick, frying pan over medium heat, add the olive oil and cook the sopes for 3 to 4 minutes on each side until golden. With a spatula, transfer them to the warm serving dish and carefully pinch the edges up with your thumb and index finger to form a tartlet – don't worry if they are not perfect, it really doesn't matter! Fill the tartlets with the refried beans, then the plantain and bacon, grated cheese and finally soured cream or yoghurt.

Serve immediately.

MASA TARTLETS WITH *CHORIZO*
Sopes de Chorizo

Plaza San Jacinto in the beautiful colonial San Ángel district of Mexico City hosts the Bazár Sábado, an open-air arts and crafts market held every Saturday. The artists set out their paintings under the trees, the craftsmen's colourful stalls fill the surrounding streets in the shadow of the magnificent Spanish mansions, and everybody, including the restaurants and street sellers, does a roaring trade. The Fonda Sán Ángel right on the square is the perfect place to relax under a sunshade, soak up the energy and buzz, watch all the comings and goings, and sample the Fonda's excellent food, which it describes as "contemporary Mexican cuisine". We started off with a large plate of typical *Antojitos Mexicanos*, reminiscent of *tapas* or Middle Eastern *mezze*. The flavours were outstanding, and these *sopes* the stars of the show.

The topping in this recipe is much more straightforward than the preceding one, but also much richer and more powerful, definitely not for delicate palates, particularly if you use Mexican chorizo. However, the blandness of the *sope* itself is a perfect partner for the savoury, deeply flavoured topping, especially if you drink some Mexican beer with it as we did at the Fonda.

Makes 4 sopes

For the sopes:-
125 g/4 ½ oz masa harina (see Resources)
30 g/1 ¼ oz wholemeal flour
15 g/½ oz butter, softened
½ tsp salt
½ tsp baking powder
175 ml/6 fl oz warm water
30 ml/2 tbsp olive oil

For the topping:-
75 g/3 oz chorizo sausage, diced
1 tbsp vegetable oil

75 g/3 oz onions, peeled and finely chopped
1 garlic clove, peeled and crushed
100 g/4 oz tomatoes, coarsely chopped
50 g/2 oz Parmesan cheese, freshly grated
60 ml/4 tbsp soured cream or Greek-style plain yoghurt
Sea salt and freshly ground black pepper

Place the masa harina, flour, butter, salt and baking powder in a food processor and process briefly. With the motor running, pour in the water and process until it is just amalgamated. Scrape into a bowl, knead into a ball, cover with clingfilm and set aside to rest for 30 minutes.

Grind the chorizo coarsely in a food processor – you don't want a purée but neither do you want big lumps.

Heat the vegetable oil in a frying pan and add the onions and garlic. Fry gently until they start to soften, about 5 minutes, then add the ground chorizo. Continue to cook until the mixture begins to brown. Stir in the tomatoes and cook until all the moisture has evaporated, about 20 minutes. At this stage, you can set the mixture aside until needed, or refrigerate it for up to 48 hours. Reheat before using.

Heat the oven to its lowest temperature, and put a serving dish to warm.

Make the sopes while the chorizo is cooking. Divide the dough into 4 balls and flatten them into circles about ¾ cm/1/3 in thick. Heat a heavy, preferably non-stick, frying pan over medium heat, add the olive oil and cook the sopes for 3 to 4 minutes on each side until golden. With a spatula, transfer them to the warm serving dish and carefully pinch the edges up with your thumb and index finger to form a tartlet – don't worry if they are not perfect, it really doesn't matter! Fill the tartlets with the chorizo mixture, sprinkle with grated cheese and drizzle with soured cream or yoghurt.

Serve immediately.

CHORIZO, PEPPER AND GOAT'S CHEESE *QUESADILLAS* WITH SMOKY *SALSA*
Quesadillas de Chorizo y Chipotle

Quesadillas are a tortilla turnover. The filling always includes cheese – *queso* is Spanish for cheese – but otherwise, the possibilities are endless, from the basic *sincronisada*, a simple cheese and ham *quesadilla*, reminiscent of a toasted cheese and ham sandwich, to the more sophisticated and often exotic combinations dished up in restaurants. They are one of the most popular street snacks – *antojitos* – served in every market *fonda* and street stall, which is undoubtedly the best place to sample them. The following recipe is my reconstruction of a *quesadilla* which we ate in the market in Oaxaca, washed down with a bottle of cold Bohemia beer.

Makes 4 quesadillas

100 g/4 oz chorizo sausage, diced
45 ml/3 tbsp olive oil
150 g/5 oz red onions, peeled and sliced
1 medium red pepper, about 175 g/6 oz, cut into 1 cm/½ in wide strips
200 g/7 oz fresh goat's cheese
100 g/4 oz Farmhouse Cheddar cheese, coarsely grated
4 corn tortillas
½ x quantity Cooked Chipotle Sauce (page 208), heated
15 g/½ oz fresh coriander, coarsely chopped
Sea salt and freshly ground black pepper

Heat a heavy dry frying pan and cook the chorizo until it has released most of its fat and is golden, about 10 minutes. With a slotted spoon, remove it to a plate lined with kitchen paper to drain. Discard the chorizo fat, wipe out the pan, pour in the olive oil and return to the heat. Add the red onions and pepper and some seasoning, and cook, stirring occasionally, until the onions are translucent and the pepper soft. The vegetables can be prepared a couple of days ahead and refrigerated.

Mix the two cheeses together.

When you are ready to cook the quesadillas, heat the oven to its lowest setting. Lay the four tortillas out on a work surface. Spread one quarter of the cheese mixture over one half of each tortilla and then one quarter of the vegetables. Fold each tortilla in half, into a half-moon shape, and press it down gently with a spatula.

Heat a large heavy frying pan and place two quesadillas in it, curved edges facing outwards. Cook them over medium heat for about 4 minutes, until lightly browned. Flip them over carefully and brown the other side. Remove to a plate and keep warm in the oven while you make the other two.

Place the quesadillas on warm plates, spoon the sauce over them, sprinkle with coriander and serve immediately.

CRAB *QUESADILLAS* LAS MAÑANITAS
Quesadillas de Jaiba Las Mañanitas

Las Mañanitas in Cuernavaca is a world of its own, a classic, a Mexican institution. When I was a child, we had a weekend house just outside Cuernavaca, and during the long school holidays, we would be treated to several visits to Las Mañanitas, where we would sit around the swimming pool, or chase each other around the lush gardens, chat to the brilliantly coloured parrots, and stalk the flamingoes, African cranes and peacocks. The children would drink *conga*, a fruit juice cocktail, while the adults knocked back the Planter's Punch – and everybody would fight over the delicious cheese and onion dip with crisps. Cuernavaca has changed beyond recognition and is no longer the quiet provincial town of my childhood. It is now a city of heavy industry, within commuting distance of the capital, its palm-lined streets choked with traffic and petrol fumes, its old charm difficult to find. But Las Mañanitas, a green oasis hidden behind its high wall, is as magical as I remember. The house belonged to the Woolworths' heiress, Barbara Hutton, and became a bijou hotel in the mid 1950s – it is elegant and gracious, discreet and surprisingly affordable, and for me at least, an experience not to be missed. The cheese and onion dip is as delicious as ever, the live music during the evening cocktail hour on the terrace as traditional and lively, the fountains and the gardens as romantic. The food in the restaurant is too international now for my taste, but these tortilla turnovers filled with crab definitely won me over. The Mexican Salad on page 210 is an excellent accompaniment, or you could simply serve them with some lightly dressed salad leaves.

Makes 4 quesadillas

160 g/5 ½ oz Boursin cheese with garlic and herbs
65 g/2 ½ oz red onions, peeled and finely chopped
1 hot red or green chilli, deseeded and finely chopped
75 g/3 oz Farmhouse Cheddar cheese, coarsely grated
2 dressed crab
20 g/¾ oz fresh coriander, coarsely chopped

4 corn tortillas
Sea salt and freshly ground black pepper

1 x quantity Mexican Salad (page 210) or mixed salad leaves, to serve

Mash the Boursin in a bowl and stir in the onions, chilli and Cheddar. Fold in the crabmeat and coriander and taste for seasoning. It may only need a bit of black pepper, as the Boursin has salt – it all depends on the saltiness of the crab.

When you are ready to cook the quesadillas, heat the oven to its lowest setting. Lay the four tortillas out on a work surface. Spread one quarter of the crab mix on one half of each tortilla. Fold each tortilla in half, into a half-moon shape, and press it down gently with a spatula.

Heat a large heavy frying pan and place two quesadillas in it, curved edges facing outwards. Cook them over medium heat for about 4 minutes, until lightly browned. Flip them over carefully and brown the other side. Remove to a plate and keep warm in the oven while you make the other two.

When all four quesadillas are cooked, place them on four warm plates, add the Mexican Salad or salad leaves, and serve immediately.

Flamingos

POTATO, *CHORIZO* AND AUBERGINE *TACOS*
Tacos de Papa, Chorizo y Berenjena

Aubergines are not native to the Americas but they are plentiful in Mexican markets, piled up beside the squashes, potatoes, chillies and tomatoes. They tend not to be used on their own, as a vegetable in their own right, but play more of a supporting role in vegetable stews or fillings. We ate these *tacos* in the market in Tepoztlán, and when I expressed my surprise at the aubergines, the cook, who cannot have been more than 15 years old, replied with a big smile: *A mi me encantan las berenjenas*, I love aubergines! The contrast of the silky aubergine against the crisp potatoes, chorizo and tortillas is wonderful and showed her to be a natural cook.

If you can't be bothered to fry the tacos, you could put a basket of warm tortillas, the vegetables, the sauce and the cheese on the table and let people make up their own…

Makes 6 tacos

700 g/1 ½ lb potatoes, scrubbed and cut into 2 cm/¾ in pieces
450 g/1 lb aubergines, cut into 2 cm/¾ in pieces
200 g/7 oz red onions, peeled and finely sliced
45 ml/3 tbsp olive oil
100 g/4 oz chorizo sausage, diced
6 corn tortillas
150 ml/¼ pint vegetable oil
1 x quantity Roast Tomato Sauce (page 204), heated
100 g/4 oz Feta cheese, crumbled
Wooden cocktail sticks
Sea salt and freshly ground black pepper

Heat the oven to 200°C/400°F/gas 6/fan oven 180°C. Cook the potatoes in boiling salted water for 10 minutes. Drain and place in a roasting tray with the aubergines and onions. Drizzle with the olive oil, season well, and roast, stirring occasionally, for one hour, until the vegetables are golden and the potatoes crusty.

While the vegetables are cooking, fry the chorizo in a heavy, dry frying pan, stirring occasionally, until it has released most of its fat and is golden, about 10 minutes. With a slotted spoon, remove it to a plate lined with kitchen paper to drain. Discard the chorizo fat and wipe out the frying pan.

When the vegetables are ready, stir the chorizo into them.

Turn the oven down to its lowest setting and put a serving dish to heat.

Lay the tortillas out on the work surface and divide the vegetable mixture between them, arranging them in a line along the middle. Roll the tortillas up firmly and secure them with a cocktail stick. Heat the vegetable oil in the chorizo frying pan until sizzling and cook the tacos until crisp all over – don't overcrowd the frying pan as you need to be able to roll the tacos around to cook them evenly. Remove the tacos to a baking tray lined with kitchen paper and keep them warm in the oven until they are all fried.

Line the tacos up side by side on the warm serving dish, pour the sauce over them and sprinkle with Feta.

Serve immediately before they go soft.

CRAB TACOS
Tacos de Jaiba

If you have some grilled tomato sauce in the freezer, these *tacos* are quick and easy to make. We ate them at a street stall in Campeche on the Gulf of Mexico – we were on our way from Palenque to Mérida, and the bus luckily stopped for an hour to enable us all to have some lunch and stretch our legs – a welcome break in the nine hour bus trip. The cook worked at mesmerising speed with nothing more than two gas burners on a table made of two wooden planks, and a large terracotta basin full of water – not much in the way of kitchen hygiene but what a natural, first-class cook she was and what wonderful ingredients were available to her: the crab was so fresh that it positively sparkled with flavour. I like to finish off the dish by placing the *tacos* under the grill for a few minutes to melt and brown the cheese.

Serves 2 generously

2 dressed crab
150 ml/¼ pint full fat crème fraîche
30 g/1 ¼ oz red onions, peeled and finely chopped
4 corn tortillas
100 ml/3 ½ fl oz vegetable oil
1 x quantity Grilled Tomato Sauce (page 204), heated
75 g/3 oz Farmhouse Cheddar or Parmesan cheese, coarsely grated
15 g/½ oz fresh coriander, coarsely chopped
1 lime, halved
Wooden cocktail sticks
Sea salt and freshly ground black pepper

Mix the crabmeat, crème fraîche, red onions and some seasoning in a bowl. Lay the tortillas out on the work surface and divide the crab mixture between them. Roll the tortillas up firmly and secure them with a cocktail stick.

Heat the vegetable oil in a heavy frying pan until sizzling. Fry the tacos for 2 or 3 minutes on each side, until crisp and golden all over – don't overcrowd the frying pan as you need to be able to roll the tacos around to cook them evenly. Drain them on kitchen paper and transfer them to a baking dish.

Heat the grill to high. Pour the sauce over the tacos and sprinkle with cheese. Grill about 10 cm/4 in from the heat for about 5 minutes, until the cheese is melted and bubbling.

Strew the coriander over the top and serve immediately with a lime half to squeeze over each portion.

SWISS *ENCHILADAS*
Enchiladas Suizas

It is difficult to know how authentic these *enchiladas* are or where Switzerland comes into the equation, but they are certainly very typical and widely available. The best ones were served at Sanborns, an American department store housed in a beautiful old tiled colonial building near the central *zócalo* in Mexico City and a favourite haunt during my teenage years. Although it is difficult to believe now that a department store could possibly be a good place to find genuine, and memorable, Mexican food, countless taxi drivers in the City recommended it to us as one of their favourite places to eat. My reply was invariably "I am a *mexicana*, not a tourist" but they remained adamant in their praise of Sanborns and its cuisine.

If you can't get hold of any *tomatillos*, the enchiladas are just as delicious with the Chipotle Chilli Sauce on page 208.

Serves 2 generously

150 ml/¼ pint double cream
1 x quantity Cooked Tomatillo Sauce (page 206)
6 corn tortillas
250 g/9 oz cooked, shredded chicken
90 g/3 ½ oz Farmhouse Cheddar cheese, coarsely grated
15 g/½ oz fresh coriander, coarsely chopped

Mix the cream into the tomatillo sauce.

Heat the oven to 200ºC/400ºF/gas 6/fan oven 180ºC.

Lay the tortillas out on the work surface and divide the chicken between them. Roll them up firmly and arrange them side by side in a baking dish. Pour the sauce over them and sprinkle with the cheese. Bake for 20 to 30 minutes, until the sauce is bubbling and the cheese melted and golden.

Strew the coriander over the top and serve immediately.

TOMATOED *TORTILLAS*
Enjitomatadas

Peasant food at its simplest, tastiest and best: a basic tomato sauce, some tortillas, a sprinkling of cheese – true poverty cooking. Every Mexican household, however poor, has tortillas (often home-made in the more rural areas), some tomato plants growing in the sun, and a goat or two tethered behind the house – in the countryside at least! *Enjitomatadas* are an intrinsic part of my past, as I had them countless times for supper when I was a child and I have never tired of them. Whole tortillas are usually used in *enjitomatada*s, dipped and folded in the sauce like Crêpes Suzette, but I find this too fiddly and messy, so I use tortilla chips instead which make the whole process infinitely easier.

Serves 2

500 g/18 oz tomatoes, halved
2 green chillies
4 garlic cloves, unpeeled
30 ml/2 tbsp olive oil
200 g/7 oz onions, peeled and coarsely chopped
1 heaped tsp bouillon powder
125 g/4 ½ oz plain tortilla chips
30 g/1 ¼ oz Parmesan cheese, freshly grated
20 g/¾ oz red onions, peeled and finely sliced
15 g/½ oz flat leaf parsley, coarsely chopped
Sea salt and freshly ground black pepper

Heat the grill to high. Line the grill pan with foil and arrange the tomatoes, cut side up, garlic and chillies in it. Grill 10 cm/4 in from the heat for 10 to 15 minutes, turning the garlic and chillies over half way through, until the tomatoes are lightly charred and caramelised. Cool then peel the garlic, and halve and deseed the chillies. Place them in a blender or food processor, add the tomatoes and some seasoning, and process to a fairly smooth purée.

Heat the olive oil in a large frying pan, add the onions, and cook over medium heat, stirring occasionally, for about 15 minutes, until soft and golden. Add the tomato purée and continue to cook for a further 10 minutes, to evaporate any excess moisture. Stir in the bouillon powder and 200 ml/7 fl oz water, lower the heat and simmer for 30 minutes. Add the tortilla chips, turning them over and over in the sauce with a large spoon until they are well coated and have softened. Pile them on to two warm plates and top with the cheese, onions and parsley.

Serve immediately.

Tortillera

TORTILLA CASSEROLES

Layered tortilla casseroles – as opposed to *chilaquiles* (page 36) – are rather like lasagne, with layers of tortillas instead of pasta.

AZTEC PUDDING
Pastel Azteca

An old school friend whom I had not seen for many years served us this tortilla casserole on our first evening in Mexico City. She gave a dinner party to welcome me back to my homeland and invited people I had not seen since I left school. It was first a tearful, and then a noisy, exuberant and unforgettable gathering, with much reminiscing and "do you remember" cropping up every few minutes. Knowing my desperate, insatiable apetite for Mexican food, my friend chose to cook us a dish full of typical ingredients. It is sharp, spicy, creamy and mellow, all at the same time. It looks complicated but it is not particularly time consuming, and both the sauce and the *rajas* can be made several days ahead. If you cannot get hold of *tomatillos*, do not hesitate to try the *Pastel* with any of the cooked tomato sauces.

Serves 4

12 corn tortillas, halved
1 large skinless, boneless chicken breast, cooked and shredded
1 x quantity Chilli Strips (page 102)
1 x quantity Cooked Tomatillo Sauce (page 206)
250 ml/8 fl oz double cream
250 g/9 oz Farmhouse Cheddar cheese, coarsely grated
1 x 1 litre/1 ¾ pint baking dish
Sea salt and freshly ground black pepper

Line the bottom of the baking dish with 8 tortilla halves, covering it completely. Arrange half the chicken on top, season it, then half the chilli strips, one third of the sauce, cream and cheese. Top with another 8 tortilla halves, the remaining chicken, some seasoning and the chilli strips, and one third of the sauce, cream and cheese.

Finish off with a final layer of tortillas, the rest of the sauce and cream, and the remaining cheese last of all.

Heat the oven to 200°C/400°F/gas 6/fan oven 180°C and bake the pudding, uncovered, for 30 minutes, until the top is crusty and the juices bubbling up around the sides.

Serve immediately.

PICADILLO TORTILLA CASSEROLE

This casserole has a distinct whiff of Italy, with its tomato and bolognese-style sauces, and its cheesy topping – but while a traditional Italian lasagna is deep and mellow, this is a rich and aromatic concoction, satisfying and soulful, smoky with *chipotle* chilli, sweet with raisins, crunchy with roasted nuts, heady with spices – infinitely more flamboyant and exotic than its European cousin.

Serves 4

For the sauce:-
2 garlic cloves, peeled
500 g/18 oz tomatoes, coarsely chopped
4 spring onions, coarsely chopped
90ml/6 tbsp olive oil
2 tsp chipotle chilli sauce (see Resources)
Sea salt

1 x quantity Picadillo (page 235)
8 corn tortillas, halved
100 g/4 oz Farmhouse Cheddar cheese, coarsely grated
1 x 1 litre/1 ¾ pint baking dish

Place all the ingredients for the sauce in a food processor and process for about 10 seconds to make a chunky purée.

Heat the oven to 200°C/400°F/gas 6/fan oven 180°C.

Spread half the sauce over the base of the baking dish. Arrange 8 tortilla halves on top, spread the Picadillo over them, followed by the remaining tortillas, the rest of the sauce and finally the cheese. Bake in the oven for 45 minutes, until the top is crusty and the juices bubbling up around the sides.

Serve immediately.

SWEETCORN HOTCAKES WITH BOURSIN *GUACAMOLE* AND SMOKED SALMON
Crepas con Guacamole y Salmón Ahumado

Smoked salmon has nothing to do with Mexico but this combination is terribly good, particularly as Boursin and Herb Roulé seem to have a real affinity to avocadoes. Smoked tuna or swordfish would actually be more authentic, but then the glorious colour combination would be lost. A Mexican cook would make crêpes rather than the thicker hotcakes and fold them over but American-style hotcakes (served for breakfast in virtually every Mexican hotel) are easier and I prefer their texture. You can make the hotcakes ahead of time and either serve them cold or reheat them in the oven, wrapped in foil; I like them warm. I make a smaller version of these hotcakes as canapés and they are always a tremendous hit.

Serves 4

For the hotcakes:-
45 ml/3 tbsp olive oil
200 g/7 oz onions, peeled and coarsely chopped
200 g/7 oz tinned or frozen sweetcorn, defrosted and well drained
250 ml/8 fl oz single cream
2 eggs
90 g/3 ½ oz polenta
75 g/3 oz plain flour
15 g/½ oz fresh coriander, coarsely chopped
1 ½ tsp sea salt
Freshly ground black pepper

For the guacamole:-
2 large, ripe avocadoes
100 g/4 oz Boursin garlic and herb cheese or Herb Roulé cheese
½ lime, juiced

400 g/14 oz smoked salmon
15 g/½ oz fresh coriander, leaves only
Sea salt and freshly ground black pepper

Heat 30 ml/2 tbsp of the olive oil in a small frying pan and cook the onions until soft and translucent, about 10 minutes. Cool and place in a food processor with the other hotcake ingredients. Process until medium smooth – keep some texture to it. Scrape the batter into a bowl and let it rest for a few minutes while you make the guacamole.

Wash the food processor. Cut the avocadoes in half, remove and reserve the stones, and scoop the flesh into the bowl of the food processor. Add the cheese, lime juice and some seasoning, and process until smooth. Scrape into a small bowl and add the avocado stones (they will prevent the guacamole from discolouring). Set aside while you make the hotcakes.

Heat the oven to its lowest setting and line a baking tray with kitchen paper. Brush a non-stick or crêpe pan with a bit of the remaining olive oil and heat until sizzling. Drop a big spoonful of the hotcake batter and spread it with the back of the spoon into a circle about 10 cm/4 in wide; let it set for a minute and then place a second spoonful of batter on top of the first – the hotcake needs to be about 1 cm/½ in thick and I find it very difficult to achieve this right from the start, as the batter just spreads too quickly. Cook until bubbles rise to the surface, then quickly flip it over with a spatula and cook for about 3 minutes longer. Remove to the baking tray and keep warm in the oven while you make 3 more hotcakes.

To serve, place the hotcakes on warm plates and top first with smoked salmon, then guacamole and finally coriander leaves.

FAJITAS

Fajitas had always struck me as being Tex-Mex rather than Mexican, so I was delighted to come across them in the Mérida market and learn that they are actually a speciality of the port of Támpico on the Gulf of Mexico. *Fajitas* are tremendous fun for an informal summer party, where you can cook it all on the BBQ and people do not mind getting their fingers sticky; this is REAL finger food.

The word *"fajita"* means "little girdle". In the case of this particular dish, which was originally made with beef, the name apparently refers to the cut of meat known in the United States as skirt steak, which is the cow's diaphragm. Chicken, fillet of lamb, pork tenderloin, chunks of monkfish and big, juicy prawns are all delicious alternatives, as are kebabs of Mediterranean vegetables, such as courgettes, peppers and aubergines. Tequila margaritas and Mexican beer with a wedge of lime in the mouth of the bottle add a final kick to the whole experience.

And if it rains on your BBQ, don't despair – just cook it all in the oven or under the grill.

The following recipes for beef, chicken and prawn *fajitas* each serve six people. If you decide to serve all three at the same time, there will be enough for eighteen but then you will need to increase the quantities of the accompaniments.

When you are ready to serve, place all the ingredients for the *fajitas* on the table so that everyone can assemble their own. Spoon the spicy meat or fish on to a warm tortilla, top with guacamole, *salsa*, refried beans, caramelised onions and soured cream, and roll it all up. Then throw caution to the winds, abandon any thought of dignity, pick the whole parcel up in your fingers and eat it as best you can! Have plenty of paper napkins available, and some knives and forks for the less adventurous.

Serves 6

For the marinade:-
4 garlic cloves, peeled and finely chopped

1 red and 1 green chilli, deseeded and finely sliced
2 tbsp red wine vinegar
1 tbsp wholegrain mustard
60 ml/4 tbsp olive oil
1 tbsp runny honey
2 tsp ground cumin
1 tsp ground cinnamon
2 tsp dried Mexican oregano (see Resources)
30 g/1 ¼ oz fresh coriander, coarsely chopped

750 g/1 ¾ lb sirloin steak
or
750 g/1 ¾ lb skinless, boneless chicken breasts
or
48 raw king prawns, shelled, deveined and threaded on to 6 metal skewers
18 corn tortillas, warmed in the oven
2 x quantities Guacamole (page 159)
2 x quantities Raw Tomato Salsa (page 201)
1 x quantity Refried Beans (page 16), heated
1 x quantity Caramelised Onions (see below), heated
600 ml/1 pint soured cream or Greek-style plain yoghurt

Make the marinade by whisking all the ingredients together with an electric beater. Place the beef, chicken or prawns in a shallow glass or china dish, pour over the marinade, cover with clingfilm and set aside in a cool place for 2 to 3 hours or overnight in the refrigerator.

Remove from the marinade and BBQ or grill the beef or chicken for 3 to 4 minutes on each side, or the prawns for 1 minute on each side, until they are just pink and firm. The prawns can be served immediately but allow the beef or chicken to rest for 5 minutes before carving into thin slices.

Wrap the beef, chicken or prawns in a warm tortilla with a spoonful of each accompaniment and eat immediately.

For the caramelised onions:-
45 ml/3 tbsp vegetable oil
750 g/1 ¾ lb red onions, peeled and finely sliced
450 ml/¾ pint Mexican beer
60 ml/4 tbsp red wine vinegar
1 tbsp runny honey
1 tsp chipotle chilli sauce (see Resources)
Sea salt and freshly ground black pepper

Heat the oil in a heavy frying pan and add the onions. Cook until soft, about 10 minutes, stirring from time to time. Add the beer, vinegar, honey and chipotle chilli sauce and simmer over low heat until the liquid has evaporated and the onions are soft, golden and caramelised. Season to taste.

The onions may be prepared up to three days ahead and refrigerated. Reheat gently before serving.

Guerrero

fire

Red and green, orange and purple, long or stubby, fat or thin: they come in all colours, shapes and sizes and look blissfully innocuous – but they conceal a heart of fire, an exuberant and unbridled passion which fills every mouthful with excitement and power. Some offer just a gentle warmth, which lingers on the taste buds; others produce an instant explosion of heat, blotting out all thought and overwhelming the mind; every one of them adds spice, fragrance and a tremendous depth and complexity of flavour to whatever it is cooked with. Chillies are the brightest star of the Mexican table.

Cooking with chillies has proved to be a real voyage of discovery, almost an adventure in consciousness. In spite of being brought up in their homeland and fed throughout my childhood by Mexican cooks, my palate has never been able to take an excess of heat – spice is one thing, fire is another! For a long time, I looked on chillies as simply being hot, hot, HOT, and associated them with inedible curries brutally flavoured with chilli powder. It is only in recent years that I have started to become better acquainted with them and embarked on a proper chilli education.

It is doubtful that my palate will ever be able cope with serious fire – just sniffing a dried *habañero* brings tears to my eyes – but my on-going learning has shown me that chillies are highly individual creatures and not merely hot: there are over 200 recorded varieties, and each one has its own personality and qualities. Furthermore, a fresh chilli will take on a totally different temperament if it is dried. Fresh chillies bring sparkle, life and vigour while dried chillies acquire wonderfully complex, mellow undertones of savour and fragrance. An old school friend gave me some invaluable advice at the start of my chilli studies: if I made a basic tomato sauce and flavoured it with a different chilli each time, I would learn to identify and appreciate that chilli's unique characteristics. The process was a real eye-opener, as I picked out the raisiny flavour of one, the nutty tones of another, or the smoky, herby bite of a third.

Countless different chillies feature in Mexican cooking, many of them very regional, even local, and little documented, but the mild *jalapeño* and the hotter *serrano* and *habañero* are the three main fresh chillies used. *Jalapeños* are low on the heat scale and leave just a hint of fire on the lips. *Serranos* are bolder, more serious, more dynamic, and can be relied on to add plenty of zing and brightness without risk of injury. *Habañeros* feature prominently in the cooking of the southern province of Yucatán and have a kick like a mule. Unless you are a real fire-eater, it is best to cook *habañeros* in a sauce, then fish them out and discard them – that way they will impart just a bearable amount of heat as well as a glorious burst of their orange, lemon and tropical fruitiness.

Poblano chillies are used more as a vegetable than a 'flavouring'. Long and buckled, they have a whisper of heat and spice, and a delicious, faintly aromatic bitterness which I love. They can be used raw in a salad, but they really shine when they are roasted or grilled until the skin blisters and chars. They are then peeled and cut into strips – *rajas* – and added to all sorts of dishes, from *enchiladas* and *quesadillas* to soups and omelettes. They are also often stuffed with a variety of fillings and then baked in a sauce – a bit fiddly but well worth the effort. My favourite partner for *poblanos* is cream; although it sounded an unlikely combination to start with, it turned out to be a marriage made in heaven. In the absence of *poblanos*, green peppers are an acceptable substitute so long as they get some warmth and support from a couple of *jalapeños* or other green chillies.

Dried chillies add a totally different dimension to the foods they are cooked with. Wizened, dark and faintly sinister-looking, they have an intensity and caramel spiciness which produce powerful, richly-flavoured sauces and stews without too great an increase in heat. Although they appear intimidating, they are actually easy to prepare: a brief toasting in a heavy frying pan, a 30-minute soak in hot water to rehydrate them, and they are ready to be puréed in a food processor – or pounded in a mortar if you are feeling energetic!

The following dried chillies are my favourites, which I have used throughout this book:-

Mulato: 3/10 on the heat scale; sweet and fruity.
Ancho: 3/10 on the heat scale; the dried version of the very Mexican *poblano* chilli,

with a rich, pruney flavour and a suggestion of heather or wild herb honey.

Guajillo: although only 3/10 on the heat scale, it can actually be unexpectedly hot and pack quite a punch. Rather tannic with faintly bitter undertones, reminiscent of cranberries and tobacco.

Pasilla: 4/10 on the heat scale; *pasilla* is Spanish for little raisin, and the *pasilla's* flavour has distinct shades of raisin and cherries, as well as a gentle acridness behind its warmth.

Chipotle: 7/10 on the heat scale, the *chipotle* is a smoked, dried *jalapeño*, rich and hot, with a distinctive flavour and hints of tobacco and chocolate. A jar of *chipotle* chilli sauce is invaluable if you do not have the time to deal with dried chillies. a spoonful will jazz up anything from a plain tomato sauce to scrambled eggs or a vinaigrette.

Habañero: 10/10 on the heat scale; intensely hot and used extensively in the cuisine of the Yucatán Peninsula. It imparts a lovely flavour of citrus and tropical fruit when added whole, and can then be fished out and discarded.

Whilst I specify particular dried chillies throughout the book, I leave the choice of fresh chillies to you, merely listing them as a "red" or "green" chilli. If you want the dish to be truly spicy, use a hot chilli; if you prefer something more delicate, go for a mild chilli. I do occasionally state a "hot" chilli if I feel the dish really requires it, but in all cases, be guided by your own palate and preference.

Cooking with chillies is certainly not for the faint-hearted but for those of us who thrive on vibrant, bold, heart-expanding food, it offers a whole new world of culinary adventure.

CHILLI AND FRUIT *SALSA*
Pico de Gallo

Pico de Gallo, meaning cockerel's beak for some unfathomable reason, is sometimes a *salsa*, sometimes a salad – we never came across the same version twice, but it always seemed to contain fruit. It also usually featured wonderfully fresh and crunchy *jícama*, a tuberous root also known as Mexican turnip with a sour-sweet, faintly starchy flavour; *jícama* is often available in large supermarkets and Caribbean shops, but since I have not so far found any in my local provincial supermarket, I use a sharp-tasting apple. This *salsa* is extremely good with grilled chicken and fish, particularly chunky kebabs like tuna or swordfish cooked on the BBQ. The chillies need to be quite hot to balance the sweetness of the fruit.

Serves 4

Seeds and juice of 1 pomegranate
2 hot green chillies, deseeded and finely chopped
2 large oranges, peeled, segmented and diced, juice reserved
1 sharp green apple, diced
50 g/2 oz red onions, peeled and finely chopped
2 garlic cloves, peeled and crushed
1 tbsp fresh lime juice, about ½ lime
15 g/½ oz mint, coarsely chopped
15 g/½ oz fresh coriander, coarsely chopped
60 ml/4 tbsp olive oil
Sea salt and freshly ground black pepper

Gently mix all the ingredients together in a small bowl. The salsa will keep its freshness and sit happily for an hour or two.

PLANTAIN SOUP WITH *CHORIZO*
Sopa de Plátano Macho con Chorizo

The flavours and textures in this soup are glorious – faintly sweet and smooth plantain, rich and savoury chorizo, spicy, raisiny chilli. It is well worth the effort to get Mexican chorizos (see Resources) but a good hot Spanish chorizo is fine. The principal actors here are the *pasilla* chillies, with their rich brown wrinkled skin and the hint of bitterness which hides behind their warmth; but beware of the *habañero* chilli cooked with the soup and never forget to remove it before puréeing, even if you are a fire-eater, as its truculence will overpower the other flavours and you will find yourself eating nothing more than a numbingly hot chilli soup.

Serves 2 generously

10 g/1/3 oz pasilla chillies (see Resources)
100 g/4 oz chorizo sausage, diced
30 ml/2 tbsp olive oil
200 g/7 oz onions, peeled and coarsely chopped
2 garlic cloves, peeled and crushed
1 habañero chilli, fresh or dried (see Resources)
1 tsp cumin seeds, coarsely ground in a mortar or spice grinder
1 tsp coriander seeds, coarsely ground in a mortar or spice grinder
2 large, ripe plantains, about 250 g/9 oz each, peeled and sliced into rounds 1 cm/½ in thick
1 litre/1 ¾ pints chicken or vegetable stock or water mixed with 1 tbsp bouillon powder
15 g/½ oz fresh coriander, coarsely chopped
Sea salt and freshly ground black pepper

Heat a small, heavy frying pan over medium heat and toast the pasilla chillies, pressing down on them with a spatula, until they start to smell aromatic. Flip them over and do the same on the other side. Cool slightly, discard the stem and seeds, and crumble on to a plate. Set aside.

Cook the chorizo over medium heat in a dry frying pan until it has released most of its fat and is golden, about 10 minutes. Add the crumbled pasilla chilli and stir-fry for 2 minutes. Remove with a slotted spoon to a plate lined with kitchen paper to drain.

Heat the olive oil in a saucepan and add the onions, garlic and habañero chilli. Cook gently, stirring occasionally, until soft and golden. Stir in the spices and some seasoning, and cook for a further 3 minutes. Add the plantain and cook, stirring occasionally, until soft and lightly browned. Pour in half the stock, bring to the boil and simmer, covered, for 20 minutes. Cool slightly, remove and discard the habañero chilli, and place the soup in a food processor. Process until smooth and return to the saucepan. Add the rest of the stock and the chorizo and chilli mix. Bring back to the boil and check the seasoning.

Ladle into two bowls and sprinkle with fresh coriander.

Serve immediately.

CHILLI STRIPS
Rajas

This is one of the most versatile and traditional of vegetable dishes. *Poblano* chillies are grilled and cut into strips, then fried with a bit of onion and garlic. They can be eaten just on their own with some warm tortillas, or mixed into any number of other dishes. I also like to use them with 'sweet' red and yellow peppers for a multi-coloured effect and a wider range of flavours – but I have to admit this is far from typical as 'sweet' peppers do not feature strongly in Mexican cooking. *Poblano* chillies are available from some larger supermarkets and by mail order (see Resources); or use 3 green peppers and some chipotle chilli sauce.

Serves 2 for lunch

650 g/1 lb 7 oz poblano chillies (see Resources) or green peppers
45 ml/3 tbsp olive oil
200 g/7 oz onions, peeled and sliced
2 garlic cloves, peeled and crushed
Chipotle chilli sauce, optional (see Resources)
Sea salt and freshly ground black pepper
Warm corn tortillas, to serve

Heat the grill to high. Line the grill pan with foil, arrange the poblano chillies or green peppers on it, and grill 10 cm/4 in from the heat, turning them as needed, until the skin is blistered and charred all over. Cool, peel, discard the stem, core and seeds and cut into long strips about 1cm/½ in wide.

While the chillies are grilling, heat the oil in a frying pan and cook the onions until soft and starting to brown, about 15 minutes. Add the garlic, the poblano strips and some seasoning, and cook on medium heat for a further 10 minutes, stirring occasionally. If you are using green peppers, add about 1 tsp of chipotle chilli sauce to give them some heat.

Serve immediately with warm tortillas.

MULTICOLOURED RAJAS
Rajas de Pimiento y Poblano

This is a gentler, sweeter version of the traditional *rajas* and considerably more colourful. *Poblano* chillies are available from some larger supermarkets and by mail order (see Resources); or use a green pepper. I often stir these *rajas* into freshly cooked spaghetti or make them into a *ciabatta* sandwich for lunch, but they are at their best in a warm, soft corn tortilla, where the faint sweetness of both the corn and the peppers brings all the flavours together. If you want to add heat without extra smokiness from the *chipotle*, a couple of mild green chillies, cut into thin strips, can be cooked with the onions – but don't make it all too hot, as this is more a soothing dish than a fiery one.

Serves 2

1 large red pepper, about 200 g/7 oz
1 large yellow or orange pepper, about 200 g/7 oz
1 large poblano chilli (see Resources) or green pepper, about 200 g/7 oz
60 ml/4 tbsp olive oil
250 g/9 oz red onions, peeled and sliced
3 garlic cloves, peeled and crushed
1 tsp chipotle chilli sauce (see Resources)
Sea salt and freshly ground black pepper
Warm corn tortillas, to serve

Heat the grill to high. Line the grill pan with foil, arrange the peppers and chilli on it, and grill about 10 cm/4 in from the heat, turning them as needed, until the skin is blistered and charred all over. Cool, peel, discard the stem, core and seeds, and cut into long strips about 1 cm/½ in wide.

Heat the oil in a frying pan and cook the onions until soft and starting to brown, about 15 minutes. Add the garlic, chipotle chilli sauce, pepper and chilli strips and some seasoning, and cook on medium heat for a further 10 minutes, stirring occasionally. Check the seasoning.

Serve immediately with warm tortillas.

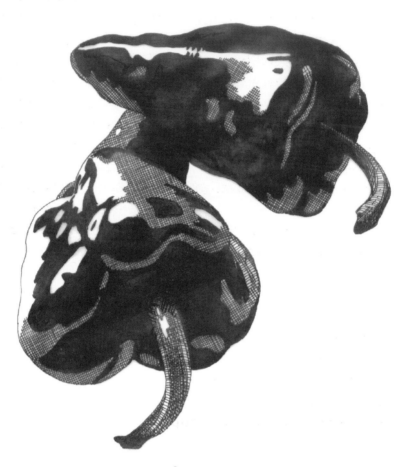

chiles poblanos

WILD MUSHROOM CRÊPES

Crepas de Hongos Silvestres

The rainy season in Mexico is short but oh so wet! I have memories of water falling from the sky in sheets so thick and solid that you could barely see across the street. And of course the rains bring mushrooms, not only the more familiar varieties such as ceps, morels, bright orange *trompetitas* and chanterelles, but more particularly the incredibly sinister-looking corn fungus, *huitlacotchle*, which grows from inside the corn kernels and blows them out into large, creepy grey lobes which crawl along the cob. I used to be terrified of it when I was small and no amount of bribes and threats would induce me to eat any dish containing it. Having more recently eaten *crêpes* with a *huitlacotchle* filling, I truly regret my childhood fears because it is the most glorious-tasting wild mushroom of all. Friends have brought me tins of *huitlacotchle* from Mexico every now and then, but they are always a bitter disappointment. However, the Mexican version of wild mushroom crêpes, with its roasted *poblano* chillies, is delicious, as are the corn-flavoured *crêpes* themselves – I have used polenta as it is more easily available than coarse *masa harina*. If you cannot get hold of any wild mushrooms, use thinly sliced portabello mushrooms – not the same but still very good.

Makes 8 crêpes

650 g/1 lb 7 oz poblano chillies (see Resources) or peppers (any colour), cut into 1 cm/½ in wide strips
60 ml/4 tbsp olive oil + 1 tsp
20 g/¾ oz dried porcini mushrooms
150 g/5 oz onions, peeled and coarsely chopped
200 g/7 oz mixed wild mushrooms, cleaned
150 ml/¼ pint double cream
1 tsp chipotle chilli sauce (see Resources)
100 g/4 oz Farmhouse Cheddar cheese, coarsely grated
Sea salt and freshly ground black pepper

For the crêpes:-
30 g/1 ¼ oz wholemeal flour

40 g/1 ½ oz polenta
1 egg
200 ml/7 fl oz milk
½ tsp sea salt

Heat the oven to 200ºC/400ºF/gas 6/fan oven 180ºC. Place the poblano or pepper strips in a roasting tin, drizzle with 2 tbsp of olive oil and roast for about 45 minutes, stirring occasionally, until they start to blacken along the edges.

Place all the ingredients for the *crêpes* in a food processor and process to a smooth batter. Pour into a jug and set aside to rest while you prepare the filling.

Put the porcini mushrooms in a small bowl and pour boiling water over them. Leave them to rehydrate for 20 minutes.

Heat the remaining 2 tbsp of olive oil in a heavy frying pan, add the onions and cook over medium heat, stirring occasionally, until soft and golden, about 15 minutes. Add the wild mushrooms and continue to cook for a further 15 minutes. Drain the porcini, reserving their liquid, and snip them into small pieces with scissors. Strain the liquid through a fine strainer, being careful to leave any sediment behind. Add the porcini and their strained liquid to the wild mushrooms, along with some seasoning. Turn the heat to high and boil briskly until most of the liquid has evaporated. Stir in the cream and chilli sauce, turn the heat right down, and simmer until thick.

Start making the crêpes while the mushrooms are cooking. Heat a small heavy frying pan over highish heat, add the 1 tsp of olive oil and wipe the pan out with a piece of kitchen paper. Pour in just enough batter to cover the bottom of the pan in a thin layer. Cook for about 1 minute, until golden and lightly set, then flip over with a palette knife and cook the other side for a further minute. Remove to a plate.

Wipe the pan again with the oily kitchen paper and repeat the process, stacking the crêpes on the plate, until you have eight of them.

By now the poblanos should be ready so remove them from the oven (leaving it on to bake the filled crêpes), stir them into the mushrooms and check the seasoning. Lay the crêpes out on a work surface and divide the filling between them. Roll them up tightly and place them side by side in a gratin dish. Sprinkle with cheese and bake in the oven for 20 minutes, until the cheese has melted and the filling is starting to bubble.

Serve immediately.

DIVORCED EGGS
Huevos Divorciados

This is certainly not a part of traditional Mexican cooking, as its origins are obviously very present-day! We ate them for breakfast in the cloister café of an old Spanish mission in beautiful San Miguel Allende, after an early morning bus journey from Guanajuato. San Miguel is an almost picture-perfect colonial town and has a large artist community – the bright, splashy colours of this dish suit it admirably. The eggs sit sullenly on opposite sides of the plate, one cloaked in red chilli sauce and its antagonist bathed in a salsa of green chillies and tomatillos – fun and very tasty. Refried beans and rice are the standard accompaniments, but the eggs are just as nice with some warm tortillas or even on toast. Both the sauces can be prepared ahead of time and refrigerated for up to three days.

Serves 2

1 x quantity Cooked Tomatillo Sauce (page 206)
1 x quantity Cooked Chipotle Chilli Sauce (page 208)
100 ml/3 ½ fl oz vegetable oil
4 eggs
1 x quantity Refried Beans (page 16), heated (optional)
Cooked rice (optional)
Sea salt and freshly ground black pepper

Warm the two sauces in two separate small saucepans.

Heat the oil in a large frying pan and fry the eggs sunny-side up. Slide them on to two warm plates, season them and top one with green sauce and one with red sauce.

Serve immediately with refried beans and rice.

CHILLI, CHICKPEA AND EGG SALAD WITH CUMIN-SPICED YOGHURT

Garbanzos con Rajas y Huevos

This is an earthy, colourful salad, aromatic and boldly flavoured. Chickpeas, like olives and capers, came to Mexico aboard the Spanish galleons and were readily welcomed into the local cuisine. They are certainly nothing like as widely used as the native *frijoles*, but they marry well with typical Mexican ingredients and perhaps make a more successful salad as they have a fairly robust texture. If you cannot find a *poblano* chilli, a green pepper will do – there will be enough heat from the red and green chillies. A Mexican cook would use soured cream but I prefer the consistency of thick yoghurt.

Serves 2 generously

1 medium-sized red pepper, about 175 g/6 oz, cut into 1 cm/½ in wide strips
1 large poblano chilli (see Resources) or green pepper, about 200 g/7 oz, cut into
1 cm/½ in wide strips
75 ml/5 tbsp olive oil
1 tbsp cumin seeds
150 ml/¼ pint Greek-style plain yoghurt
1 x 400 g/14 oz tin chickpeas, drained and rinsed
40 g/1 ½ oz red onions, peeled and finely chopped
1 garlic clove, peeled and crushed
100 g/4 oz red cherry tomatoes, quartered
1 tbsp capers, rinsed, squeezed dry and coarsely chopped
20 g/¾ oz black olives, pitted and halved
15 g/½ oz flat leaf parsley, coarsely chopped
15 g/½ oz fresh coriander, coarsely chopped
1 red and 1 green chilli, deseeded and finely sliced
2 eggs, hardboiled, peeled and quartered
Sea salt and freshly ground black pepper

Start by roasting the pepper and poblano chilli, as this can be done well ahead of time. Heat the oven to 180°C/350°/gas 4/fan oven 160°C. Place the pepper and chilli strips in a small baking dish, drizzle with 1 tbsp of olive oil, sprinkle with salt and pepper, and bake for about 40 minutes, stirring occasionally, until soft and slightly blackened along the edges. Cool and set aside until needed.

Toast the cumin seeds in a heavy frying pan over medium heat, stirring all the time, until they release their aroma – 2 to 3 minutes. Grind them coarsely in a mortar or spice grinder, then whisk them into the yoghurt with some salt and 1 tbsp of olive oil. Set aside.

Place the roasted poblano and pepper strips, chickpeas, red onions, garlic, tomatoes, capers, olives, herbs, chillies and remaining olive oil in a roomy bowl. Season well and mix gently.

Pile the salad onto a large flat serving dish, garnish with the egg and serve with the yoghurt.

MELTED CHEESE WITH *CHORIZO* AND PEPPERS
Queso Fundido

I have cheated slightly with this recipe by making it into a sort of gratin with the *chorizo* and peppers underneath the cheese. It is an incredibly savoury, if somewhat indigestible, combination and the restaurant in Oaxaca where we ate it served it all separately: *chorizo*, *poblano* chillies, and an earthenware dish of bubbling, hissing, runny cheese. The little waitress explained to us how to layer it up in a soft, warm tortilla – it was quite wonderful. I find that putting it all in the one dish is easier and keeps it from getting cold too quickly. I have also tried baking it in the oven rather than placing it under the grill, but the result was rather greasy. If you cannot get hold of a *poblano* chilli, substitute a green pepper. I use hot fresh chillies with this dish to balance the extreme richness of the cheese.

Serves 2/4

225 g/8 oz chorizo sausage, diced
300 g/11 oz onions, peeled and sliced
1 large poblano chilli (see Resources) or green pepper, about 200 g/7 oz, cut into 1 cm/½ in wide strips
1 large red pepper, about 200 g/7 oz, cut into 1 cm/½ in wide strips
1 large yellow or orange pepper, about 200 g/7 oz, cut into 1 cm/½ in wide strips
30 ml/2 tbsp olive oil
2 hot red or green chillies, deseeded and finely sliced
1 tsp dried Mexican oregano (see Resources)
300 g/11 oz Farmhouse Cheddar cheese, coarsely grated
Warm corn tortillas, to serve
Sea salt and freshly ground black pepper

Cook the chorizo in a heavy dry frying pan over medium heat until it has released most of its fat and is golden, about 10 minutes. With a slotted spoon, remove it to a plate lined with kitchen paper to drain.

Heat the oven to 200°C/400°F/gas 6/fan oven 180°C. Place the onions, poblano and peppers in a gratin dish, drizzle with olive oil and season well. Bake for 15 minutes. Add the two chillies and cook for a further 15 minutes, stirring occasionally, until the onions are golden and the peppers are just starting to blacken along the edges. Stir in the oregano and chorizo and remove from the oven.

Heat the grill to high. Spread the grated cheese over the pepper mixture, place it under the grill and cook until bubbling and golden.

Serve immediately, spooned into warm tortillas – but be careful, the cheese will be very hot!

ROAST VEGETABLES IN PUMPKIN SEED SAUCE
Verduras en Pipián

While I have used traditional Mexican vegetables in this recipe, winter vegetables such as celeriac, swede, turnips and parsnips are all delicious with this very pre-Hispanic Mexican sauce – their innate sweetness offsets the smoky spiciness of the *chipotle*. Pumpkin seeds, *pepitas*, are a traditional Mexican ingredient used to thicken sauces and their bright green oil is highly prized; they need to be lightly cooked in a dry frying pan before being ground and their toasty richness lends an indefinable, deeply satisfying flavour to anything they partner. The vegetables make a lovely vegetarian supper dish with some bread or tortillas and a salad.

Serves 4

250 g/9 oz red potatoes, scrubbed and cut into 2 cm/¾ in pieces
300 g/11 oz sweet potatoes, peeled and cut into 2 cm/¾ in pieces
250 g/9 oz courgettes, topped, tailed and sliced into 1 cm/½ in rounds
150 g/5 oz baby sweetcorn
60 ml/4 tbsp olive oil
175 g/6 oz hulled pumpkin seeds
1 x quantity Cooked Chipotle Chilli Sauce (page 208)
Sea salt and freshly ground black pepper

Heat the oven to 200°C/400°F/gas 6/fan oven 180°C. Place the vegetables in a large roasting pan, drizzle with the olive oil and season well. Roast them for about one hour, stirring occasionally, until they are soft and golden in places.

While the vegetables are roasting, put the pumpkin seeds in a heavy frying pan over medium heat and cook, stirring constantly, until they pop and just start to brown – 4 to 5 minutes. Be careful not to let them scorch or the sauce will be bitter. Cool slightly and set 2 tbsp aside for the garnish. Grind the remainder finely in a food processor.

Heat the chilli sauce in a medium saucepan and stir in the ground pumpkin seeds just before serving.

When the vegetables are ready, transfer them to a serving dish, pour the sauce over them and garnish with the whole pumpkin seeds.

Serve immediately.

ROAST VEGETABLE AND CHORIZO *TINGA*
Tinga de Verduras y Chorizo

Tinga Poblana is a speciality of the colonial city of Puebla, a real gastronomic centre – the famous *mole poblano* (see page 246) is considered Mexico's national dish. *Tinga* refers essentially to the tomato and chilli sauce but anything cooked in it seems to become a *tinga*. We ate several different versions while we were in the area, all of which contained pork in one shape or another, but also chicken and on one occasion beef. This particular recipe is based on a vegetable *tinga* we ate in Cholula, which was made with potatoes rather than aubergines. My experiments in my own kitchen resulted in a stew of ratatouille-style vegetables which I have flavoured *a la poblana*. The faint sweetness of the plantains works fabulously with the smokiness of the chilli and the savoury cheese and *chorizo*. If you cannot find a *poblano* chilli, substitute a green pepper.

Serves 4

300 g/11 oz onions, peeled and sliced
350 g/12 oz aubergines, cut into 2.5 cm/1 in pieces
350 g/12 oz courgettes, sliced into 1 cm/½ in rounds
1 medium red pepper, about 175 g/6 oz, cut into 1 cm/½ in wide strips
1 medium yellow pepper, about 175 g/6 oz, cut into 1 cm/½ in wide strips
1 large poblano chilli (see Resources) or green pepper, about 200 g/7 oz, cut into 1 cm/½ in wide strips
90 ml/6 tbsp olive oil
750 g/1 ¾ lb tomatoes, halved
3 large garlic cloves, unpeeled
1 tbsp chipotle chilli sauce (see Resources)
100 ml/3 ½ fl oz vegetable oil
2 ripe plantains, about 250 g/9 oz each, peeled and sliced into 1 cm/½ in rounds
225 g/8 oz chorizo sausage, diced
100 g/4 oz Feta cheese
15 g/½ oz mint, coarsely chopped
Warm tortillas or crusty bread, to serve

Heat the oven to 220°C/425°F/gas 7/fan oven 200°C. Place the onions, aubergines, courgettes, peppers and poblano chilli in a baking dish, season well and drizzle with 4 tbsp of olive oil. Roast in the oven for one hour, stirring every 15 minutes.

While the vegetables are roasting, heat the grill to high. Line the grill pan with foil and place the tomatoes cut side up on it. Tuck the garlic cloves in among them, and grill about 10 cm/4 in from the heat for 15 to 20 minutes, turning the garlic over half way through, until the tomatoes are blistered and starting to blacken and the garlic is brown and soft. Cool slightly then peel the garlic cloves and place them, with the tomatoes, their juices and the chilli sauce, in a food processor. Process to a chunky purée.

Heat the vegetable oil in a heavy non-stick frying pan and add the slices of plantain in one layer, browning them quickly on both sides – keep them moving around in the oil as they stick easily. With a slotted spoon, remove them to a plate lined with kitchen paper to drain.

Add the chorizo to the frying pan and cook over medium heat until it has released most of its fat and is golden, about 10 minutes. With a slotted spoon, remove it to a plate lined with kitchen paper to drain.

Discard the fat from the pan and wipe it clean. Return it to the heat, add the remaining olive oil and the tomato sauce and simmer for 15 minutes. Add the chorizo and the roasted vegetables and bring back to a simmer. Check the seasoning, crumble over the Feta, top with plantain and sprinkle with chopped mint.

Serve immediately with tortillas or crusty bread to mop up all the wonderful juices.

La Catedral, Puebla

SWEETCORN BAKE WITH CREAMY RAJAS
Budín de Elote con Rajas y Crema

This is a rich, utterly heavenly combination – the silky, faintly spicy rajas with the sweetness of the corn and the graininess of the bake. Savoury puddings – *budines* – are very popular in Mexico and tend to be served as a vegetable course on their own, after a soup and before the main course, but they are decidedly filling so I prefer to have my *budín* as a lunch or supper dish with nothing more than a salad. Leftovers are also very good cold, although somewhat solid.

Serves 4

50 g/2 oz butter
200 g/7 oz red onions, peeled and coarsely chopped
2 garlic cloves, peeled and crushed
550 g/1 ¼ lb tinned or frozen sweetcorn, defrosted and well drained
250 ml/8 fl oz milk
4 eggs, lightly beaten
15 g/½ oz flat leaf parsley, very coarsely chopped
125 g/4 ½ oz Farmhouse Cheddar cheese, coarsely grated
1 tsp sea salt
1 tsp baking powder
1 x quantity Multicoloured Rajas (page 103)
250 ml/8 fl oz double cream
1 x l litre/1 ¾ pints baking dish, lightly buttered
Freshly ground black pepper

Melt the butter in a small frying pan and cook the onions and garlic until soft and lightly browned, about 15 minutes.

Heat the oven to 200°C/400°F/gas 6/fan oven 180°C.

Process about half the sweetcorn with the milk in a food processor, stopping to scrape down the sides of the bowl, until fairly smooth. Add the eggs and parsley and process again. Transfer to a large bowl and stir in the remaining sweetcorn, cheese, salt, baking powder and some black pepper, and pour into the baking dish.

Cook in the oven for 45 minutes, until firm and golden.

Prepare the rajas while the bake is cooking. When they are ready, add the cream to them in the frying pan and simmer very gently for about 20 minutes. Check the seasoning.

Serve the bake with the rajas.

SCRAMBLED EGG AND *CHORIZO TACOS*
Tacos de Huevo con Chorizo

A popular breakfast dish at the market and street stalls: *huevos a la mexicana* (Mexican eggs) given a blast of extra oomph from the chorizo and rolled into a warm tortilla with a spoonful of spicy, savoury *rajas* – certainly an energising start to the day! We also came across the eggs with a spiky crown of *totopos*, tortilla chips, instead of the tortilla, rather like the *Migas* on page 55, and the chilli strips served on the side; and with bacon, *tocino*, instead of the chorizo, which is just as aromatic and less spicy if you prefer something slightly more delicately seasoned.

Serves 2

100 g/4 oz chorizo sausage, diced
1 tbsp olive oil
100 g/4 oz onions, peeled and coarsely chopped
1 hot green chilli, deseeded and coarsely chopped
125 g/4 ½ oz tomatoes, coarsely chopped
4 eggs, lightly beaten
1 x quantity Chilli Strips (page 102)
4 corn tortillas
Sea salt and freshly ground black pepper

Cook the chorizo in a dry frying pan over medium heat, stirring often, until it has released its fat and is golden, about 10 minutes. With a slotted spoon, remove it to a plate lined with kitchen paper to drain.

Discard the fat and wipe out the frying pan. Return it to the heat and add the olive oil. Stir in the onions and chilli, and cook gently, over low heat, until soft and translucent, about 10 minutes. Add the tomatoes and some seasoning and cook for another 10 to 15 minutes, until the they are soft and most of their moisture has evaporated. Stir in the chorizo.

Heat the oven to its lowest setting. Place the rajas in a small baking dish and put them in the oven to heat. Wrap the tortillas in foil and place them in the oven as well.

Pour the eggs into the tomatoes and chorizo and cook gently, stirring often, until they are softly scrambled. Check the seasoning.

To serve, place a good spoonful of egg on a warm tortilla, top with some rajas, roll up and eat forthwith.

RICE CASSEROLE
Cazuela de Arroz

The Spanish origins of this dish are fairly evident – a sort of Mexican *paella*, but that much richer, spicier and soupier. Countless versions of *cazuela* are served all along the Mexican coast, flavoured with whatever seafood or fish is available that day, whatever the local sausage is, whatever bit of meat the cook bought at the market that morning. Brown rice is not used in traditional Mexican cooking, but its chewy texture works well here, particularly if it is brown basmati. I normally discard the fat from *chorizo* sausages but it adds very considerably to the flavour of this dish so I forget about my heart and its health in this instance!

Serves 4

30 ml/2 tbsp olive oil
2 chicken thighs
2 chicken drumsticks
100 g/4 oz chorizo sausage, diced
350 g/12 oz onions, peeled and chopped
1 large red pepper, about 200 g/7 oz, cut into 1 cm/½ in strips
1 large yellow pepper, about 200 g/7 oz, cut into 1 cm/½ in strips
200 g/7 oz long grain brown rice
200 g/7 oz raw king prawns, shelled and deveined
15 g/½ oz fresh coriander, coarsely chopped
Sea salt and freshly ground black pepper

For the salsa:-
50 g/2 oz red onions, peeled and coarsely chopped
2 hot green chillies, halved and deseeded
2 garlic cloves, peeled and halved
60 ml/4 tbsp olive oil
500 g/18 oz tomatoes, quartered
Sea salt and freshly ground black pepper

Heat the olive oil in a large frying pan, add the chicken and brown on all sides.

Remove to a plate and set aside. Add the chorizo, onions and peppers to the frying pan and cook, stirring every now and then, for 20 minutes.

For the salsa, place the onions, chillies, garlic and olive oil in a food processor and process until fairly finely chopped. Add the tomatoes and some seasoning and whiz for a few seconds, to break them down a bit without puréeing them.

Cook the rice in plenty of boiling, salted water for 45 minutes. Drain well and return to the saucepan to keep warm, covered with a dishcloth and the saucepan lid, while the rest of the dish finishes cooking.

Add the salsa and the chicken with any juices to the onion mixture in the frying pan and cook on low heat, partially covered, for a further 45 minutes, until most of the moisture has evaporated. Add the prawns and some salt and pepper and stir-fry it all until they just turn pink, about 3 minutes. Stir in the rice, mix well and continue to stir-fry for a further 5 minutes. Check the seasoning.

Serve immediately, sprinkled with coriander.

Cazuela de arroz

SPAGHETTI WITH CRAB AND *GUACAMOLE*

Sopa Seca de Jaiba

Sopa seca is such a strange expression. It means dry soup and is often used to describe rice and pasta dishes, which are served between the first and main courses. Although I remembered *sopa seca* from my childhood, I innocently ordered this dish at a beach side restaurant on the Caribbean coast and sat back to await my crab and avocado soup – needless to say, it was not a soup at all, but a large plate of thin spaghetti mixed with wonderfully fresh crab and positively sparkling with lime juice, chilli and coriander. The guacamole came in a separate bowl and we were instructed to add spoonfuls of it to the pasta as we ate.

It is essential that you use pristinely fresh crab, so if all you can lay your hands on is frozen, let alone tinned, leave this recipe for another day.

Serves 2

50 g/2 oz red onions, peeled and finely chopped
1 garlic clove, peeled and crushed
1 large red chilli, deseeded and finely sliced
1 large green chilli, deseeded and finely sliced
30 ml/2 tbsp fresh lime juice, about 1 large lime
45 ml/3 tbsp olive oil
200 g/7 oz spaghetti
2 dressed crab
15 g/½ oz flat leaf parsley, coarsely chopped
Sea salt and freshly ground black pepper

1 x quantity Guacamole (page 159) without chillies or tomatoes

Mix the onions, garlic, chillies, lime juice and olive oil in a small bowl.

Bring a large pan of salted water to the boil and cook the spaghetti according to the manufacturer's instructions. Drain well and return to the saucepan. Stir in the contents of the bowl and some seasoning, and then gently fold in the crabmeat.

Divide the pasta between two warm bowls, sprinkle with the parsley, top with some guacamole and serve immediately. Add more guacamole to the spaghetti as you eat.

BAKED *ACHIOTE* SWORDFISH

Pez Espada Pibil

Baking meat and fish in a *pib* – a stone-lined pit – is a traditional Mayan cooking method. The food is slathered with an earthy spice marinade, wrapped in banana leaves, and cooked underground, buried beneath a layer of wet leaves and earth, until tender. We were disappointed not to come across any really authentic *pibil* dishes in the Yucatán, but as several market cooks informed me, it is a time-consuming and convoluted process which does not fit in well with 21st century life anywhere. However, we were able to sample a modern version of chicken and fish *pibil* on several occasions – both baked in an ordinary oven and cooked on a BBQ.

Achiote is known as the saffron of Mexico: the fruit of this native shrub contains bright pink *annatto* seeds, which are extremely hard and therefore difficult to grind, but their earthy, mellow flavour is quite wonderful. Banana leaves can usually be found in Oriental shops, but since I cannot purchase them locally, I wrap the swordfish in kitchen foil – not the same, as the banana leaves do add an elusive tropical herbiness, but still extremely good.

Serves 4

1 tsp anatto seeds (see Resources)
½ tsp sea salt
½ tsp black peppercorns
1 tsp cumin seeds
½ tsp coriander seeds
½ tsp allspice berries
½ tsp dried Mexican oregano (see Resources)
½ tsp ground cinnamon
¼ tsp ground cloves
3 garlic cloves, peeled and crushed
30 ml/2 tbsp fresh orange juice, about ½ orange
15 ml/1 tbsp fresh lime juice, about ½ lime
30 ml/2 tbsp olive oil

4 swordfish steaks
1 x quantity Chilli and Fruit Salsa (page 99)

Place the annatto seeds and salt in an electric spice grinder and grind finely, stopping every so often to scrape down the sides of the grinder. Add the remaining spices and grind finely again. Transfer the spice powder to a small bowl and add the garlic, orange and lime juices, and olive oil. Mix well.

Lay the swordfish out on a large plate and smear the spice mix liberally on both sides. Set aside to marinate for a couple of hours.

Heat the oven to 200°C/400°F/gas 6/fan oven 180°C.

Cut out four squares of foil large enough to enclose the swordfish steaks completely. Transfer the steaks to the foil, spoon any marinade remaining on the plate on top of them, and wrap them well. Bake the fish in the oven for 15 minutes.

Place the packages on four warm plates and be ready for the fantastic aroma which will waft out of them as you unwrap them!

Serve immediately with the Chilli and Fruit Salsa.

GRILLED TUNA IN PUMPKIN SEED SAUCE
Atún en Pipián

Pumpkins originated in the Americas and the seeds were used not only to thicken sauces, but also to provide body, protein, a glorious aroma and an extra layer of nutty savouriness. This sauce is deceptively simple in that the toasting gives the seeds a wonderfully rich, mellow flavour which is quite unexpected – not just a tomato sauce, not just a chilli sauce, but a sauce with a hint of exoticism and mystery that is difficult to pin down. It also goes exceptionally well with roasted vegetables (see page 113).

Serves 4

175 g/6 oz hulled pumpkin seeds
1 x quantity Cooked Chipotle Chilli Sauce (page 208)
4 fresh tuna steaks, about 175 g/6 oz each and 1 cm/½ in thick
1 tbsp olive oil
Sea salt and freshly ground black pepper

Place the pumpkin seeds in a heavy frying pan over medium heat and cook, stirring constantly, until they pop and just start to brown – 4 to 5 minutes. Be careful not to let them scorch or the sauce will be bitter. Cool slightly and set 2 tbsp aside for the garnish. Grind the remainder finely in a food processor.

Heat the chilli sauce in a medium saucepan. Stir in the ground pumpkin seeds just before serving.

Brush the tuna steaks with olive oil and season them. Cook them on a cast iron griddle or on a BBQ for about 2 minutes on each side – tuna needs to be rare in the middle. With a spatula, transfer the steaks to four warm plates, pour the sauce over them and garnish with the reserved pumpkin seeds.

Serve immediately.

GUAJILLO CHILLI PRAWNS
Camarones con Guajillos

Guajillo chillies are medium hot, with a distinct aroma of cranberries and tobacco, and a pleasant bitterness. They are brick red when re-hydrated and, in this sauce, are paired with spices and sweet onions to showcase their very specific flavour. I find that there is no point in using them in a traditional tomato-based sauce because their personality simply vanishes and all that is left is their heat. The acidity of tomatoes also seems to accentuate their bitterness, giving the sauce a rather unpleasant, hard edge. The sharp richness of crème fraîche or soured cream on the other hand brings out their fruit and sassiness. It is always essential to strain any sauce made with *guajillos* as their skin is hard and does not break down when puréed, leaving you with horrid, sharp bits to spit out. These prawns are particularly good as a spaghetti sauce.

Serves 2

50 g/2 oz guajillo chillies (see Resources)
1 tsp cumin seeds
1 tsp dried Mexican oregano (see Resources)
60 ml/4 tbsp olive oil
350 g/12 oz onions, peeled and coarsely chopped
4 garlic cloves, peeled and crushed
125 ml/4 ½ fl oz full-fat crème fraîche or soured cream
400 g/14 oz raw king prawns, shelled and deveined
15 g/½ oz fresh coriander, coarsely chopped
Runny honey
Sea salt and freshly ground black pepper
Cooked spaghetti or warm corn tortillas, to serve

Heat a heavy frying pan over medium heat and toast the chillies, pressing down on them with a spatula, until they start to smell aromatic, about 3 minutes. Flip them over and do the same on the other side. Place them in a bowl, cover with boiling water, put a small saucepan lid or plate on top to keep them submerged, and set them aside to soak for 30 minutes. Drain and discard the stem, ribs and seeds. Place them in a food processor, add 100 ml/3 ½ fl oz of water and process until you have a thick, brick-red sauce. Strain through a medium mesh sieve to remove the bits of skin.

Toast the cumin seeds in a heavy frying pan over medium heat, stirring all the time, until they release their aroma – 2 to 3 minutes. Transfer to a mortar, add the oregano and grind it all together with a pestle – you can use an electric spice grinder if you prefer but keep some texture to it, you do not want dry powder.

Heat the olive oil in a frying pan and cook the onions and garlic until soft and golden. Add the spice mix and cook for 1 minute, then add the chilli purée, the crème fraîche and some salt and pepper, and cook over medium heat for about 10 minutes, stirring often, until nice and thick. Check the seasoning and if the sauce is a tiny bit bitter for you, squeeze in some honey – but not too much as you do not want to mask the flavour of the guajillos. Add the prawns and cook, stirring, just until the prawns turn pink, 3 or 4 minutes.

Sprinkle with coriander and serve immediately atop freshly cooked spaghetti or with warm tortillas.

CHICKEN IN RED *PIPIÁN* SAUCE

Pollo en Pipián Rojo

A *pipián* is Mexican food at its most authentic, and most historical, a real pre-Conquest dish. In fact, leave out the onions, which were a Spanish import, and you will be left with the type of sauce, thickened with seeds or nuts, which the Spaniards found bubbling in the earthenware pots of the market in Tenochtitlán. Sometimes the name applies to an absolutely basic sauce, consisting of nothing much more than the toasted seeds or nuts and some stock or even water; but it can also be richly flavoured with spices and chillies, and further enhanced by the acidity of tomatoes or tomatillos. This particular version features raisiny *ancho* chillies, a bit of smoky *chipotle*, and the mellowness of toasted sesame seeds – and here I am not being in the least bit authentic, in that I am using *tahini*, the Middle Eastern sesame paste. A Mexican cook would toast sesame seeds in a heavy frying pan and then grind them finely; but I have found that dark *tahini* works extremely well and saves me a considerable amount of trouble and washing up.

Serves 4

50 g/2 oz ancho chillies (see Resources)
250 ml/8 fl oz strong chicken stock, or water and a chicken stock cube
8 garlic cloves, unpeeled
500 g/18 oz tomatoes, halved
1 tbsp olive oil
1 chicken, jointed into 8 pieces
175 g/6 oz onions, peeled and coarsely chopped
½ tsp ground cloves
1 tsp ground cinnamon
1 tsp honey
1 tbsp chipotle chilli sauce (see Resources)
100 ml/3 ½ fl oz dark tahini (sesame paste)
1 tbsp wine or cider vinegar
15 g/½ oz fresh coriander, coarsely chopped
Sea salt and freshly ground black pepper

Heat a heavy frying pan over medium heat and toast the chillies, pressing down on them with a spatula, until they start to smell aromatic, about 3 minutes. Flip them over and do the same on the other side. Place them in a bowl, cover with boiling water, put a small saucepan lid or plate on top to keep them submerged and set them aside to soak for 20 minutes. Drain them, discard the stems, seeds and ribs, and place them in a food processor. Add the stock and process until smooth, Strain the purée through a medium mesh sieve to get rid of any bits of skin. Rinse out the food processor as you will need it for the tomatoes.

While the chillies are soaking, heat the grill to high. Line the grill pan with foil, arrange the garlic and tomatoes, cut side up, on it and grill about 10 cm/4 in from the heat for 10 to 15 minutes, turning the garlic once half way through. The garlic should be brown and soft, and the tomatoes starting to blacken around the edges. Set aside until the garlic is cool enough to handle.

Heat the heavy frying pan again, add the olive oil, and cook the chicken pieces all over until nicely browned. Remove to a plate with a spatula or kitchen tongs and set aside. Add the onions to the frying pan and cook, stirring occasionally, until soft and brown. Sprinkle in the spices and stir-fry for a couple of minutes, then pour in the chilli purée. Stir well, turn down the heat and simmer for 10 minutes.

Peel the garlic cloves and process them with the tomatoes and any juices in a food processor to a fairly smooth purée. Add to the chilli sauce in the frying pan, along with the honey, chipotle chilli sauce, tahini, vinegar and some seasoning. Place the chicken pieces on top, cover the pan and simmer gently until the chicken is tender, about 40 minutes.

Check the seasoning, sprinkle with coriander and serve immediately.

El Olmeca

ROAST DUCK WITH *MULATO* CHILLIES
Pato en Adobo de Mulatos

An *adobo* is a pure chilli sauce – I say pure because unlike most chilli sauces, it does not contain tomatoes. It is based on a purée of dried chillies, flavoured with herbs and spices, and sharpened with vinegar or citrus juice. Any dried chillies can be used, but I have opted here for the faintly sweet and fruity *mulato* which partners the richness of the duck very elegantly, producing a swarthy-looking, deeply savoury sauce. On the other hand, *mulatos* are low on the heat scale, and if you prefer something punchier, do not hesitate to use the same weight of the hotter *pasillas* or *guajillos*, or to add a bit of *chipotle* chilli sauce at the end.

Serves 2

1 duck, about 2 kg/4 ½ lb, with giblets
50 g/2 oz mulato chillies (see Resources)
30 ml/2 tbsp olive oil
275 g/10 oz onions, peeled and coarsely chopped
3 garlic cloves, peeled and coarsely chopped
1 tsp ground cinnamon
1 tsp cumin seeds, coarsely ground in a mortar or spice grinder
1 tsp soft brown sugar
1 tsp sea salt
1 tsp wine or cider vinegar

Place the duck giblets in a small saucepan, add about 500 ml/1 pint of water and simmer for a couple of hours to make a stock.

Heat a heavy frying pan over medium heat and toast the chillies, pressing down on them with a spatula, until they start to smell aromatic, about 3 minutes. Flip them over and do the same on the other side. Place them in a bowl, cover with boiling water, put a small saucepan lid or plate on top to keep them submerged and set them aside to soak for 30 minutes.

Heat 1 tbsp of the olive oil in a frying pan and cook the onions and garlic over low heat, stirring occasionally, until soft and golden.

When the chillies are ready, drain them, discard the stems, seeds and ribs, and place them in a food processor with the onions and garlic, remaining olive oil, spices, sugar, salt and vinegar. Process to a fairly smooth paste, adding a little water if necessary.

Heat the oven to 200°C/400°F/gas 6/fan oven 180°C. Sit the duck in a heavy roasting tin and rub half the chilli paste all over it. Roast it for 2 hours, basting with the fat and juices every 20 minutes or so. Remove from the oven and turn the oven off. Place the duck on a serving dish and return it to the oven with the door ajar while you make the sauce.

Strain the duck stock into a measuring jug. You should have about 250 ml/8 fl oz but if there is less, add some water.

Carefully pour off as much of the duck fat from the roasting tin as you can so that you are left with the dark and syrupy meat juices. Place the roasting tin on the hob over medium heat, pour in the duck stock and bring to the boil, scraping all the crusty bits off the bottom of the tin. Stir in the remaining chilli purée and taste for seasoning, adding a bit more sugar, salt or vinegar if necessary.

Carve the duck and serve immediately with the sauce – the skin will be absolutely delicious.

STUFFED PEPPERS
Chiles Rellenos

Poblano chillies would be used in Mexico, but apart from the easier availability of sweet peppers, I like the splash of colour. *Chiles Rellenos* are as Mexican as you can get – they are served regularly in every home, restaurant and *fonda*, more as a snack than a main course. The stuffing can vary: we had them filled with mixed vegetables in Puebla (a bit dull), squash blossoms and runny, stringy cheese in the Sán Juán market in Mexico City (wonderfully rich), salt cod on the Pacific coast (nothing like rich enough), or spicy, savoury, gutsy *picadillo*, which really does make it into a main course if you serve a pepper per person.

Serves 2/4

1 large red pepper, about 200 g/7 oz
1 large yellow pepper, about 200 g/7 oz
30 ml/2 tbsp olive oil
1 x quantity Picadillo (page 235)
200 g/7 oz Feta cheese
1 x quantity Raw Tomato Salsa (page 201)

Heat the oven to 200°C/400°F/gas 6/fan oven 180°C.

Cut the peppers in half, discard the stem, core and seeds, and place them cut side up in a baking dish where they fit snugly. Drizzle the olive oil over them, season them, cover the dish with foil, and bake in the oven for one hour. Remove the foil, fill the peppers with Picadillo, crumble the Feta cheese over them, and return them to the oven for a further 20 minutes.

With a wide spatula, transfer them carefully to warm plates, spoon some salsa over the top and serve immediately, with the rest of the salsa on the side.

MEATBALLS IN *CHIPOTLE* CHILLI SAUCE
Albóndigas en Chipotle

Leave out the chilli in the sauce and you have a traditional Italian dish. In fact, I usually serve these wonderfully savoury meatballs with pasta but rice would be more traditional. You can also add some hot stock to thin out the sauce and make it into a soup, in which case very thin pasta – *fideos* – would be totally traditional. And if you would like some extra heat, don't hesitate to add a chopped fresh chilli to the meatball mixture at the processing stage.

Serves 4

1 large red pepper, about 200 g/7 oz
75 g/3 oz onions, peeled and coarsely chopped
30 g/1 ¼ oz wholemeal bread, weighed without crusts
20 g/¾ oz grated Parmesan cheese
1 tsp sea salt
1 egg
15 g/½ oz flat leaf parsley, coarsely chopped
400 g/14 oz minced lamb

For the sauce:-
1 kg/2 ¼ lb tomatoes, halved
6 large garlic cloves, peeled and finely sliced
2 tsp runny honey
30 ml/2 tbsp olive oil
1 tbsp chipotle chilli sauce (see Resources)
Sea salt and freshly ground black pepper

Heat the grill to high. Line the grill pan with foil, place the red pepper on it, and grill about 10 cm/4 in from the heat, turning as needed, until the skin is blackened and blistered on all sides. Cool, peel, discard the stem, core and seeds and cut the flesh into small dice.

Place the onions, bread, Parmesan cheese, salt, egg and parsley in a food processor and process until finely chopped. Scrape into a bowl and stir in the lamb and the cooled red pepper. Shape into meatballs about 4 cm/1 ½ in across and arrange in a baking dish. Refrigerate for at least one hour and bring back to room temperature before cooking.

For the sauce, heat the oven to 200°C/400°F/gas 6/fan oven 180°C. Put the tomatoes cut side up in a roasting tin lined with foil and push the garlic slivers into the seedy parts. Drizzle first with honey and then olive oil. Season well and cook for one to one and a half hours, until soft and slightly blackened. Remove from the oven, leaving it on, and cool the tomatoes for 10 minutes. Place them in a food processor with the chipotle chilli sauce and process until smooth. Check the seasoning.

Pour the sauce over the meatballs and bake in the oven for 15 minutes.

Serve immediately.

MARINATED LAMB CHOPS WITH SMOKY LENTILS
Costillas con Lentejas Enchipotladas

The chilli marinade permeates the meat with a hint of smoke and herbed spice, perfect partners to the faint sweetness of lamb. I often use the same marinade as a dressing for shredded left-over roast lamb, which I then wrap with the lentils in a warm, soft corn tortilla to make an incredibly delicious *taco*. Lamb does not seem to be widely available in Mexico, although we spotted plenty of sheep in the countryside, so it was quite a surprise to be served this dish in Cuernavaca, admittedly at a rather touristy restaurant.

Serves 2

For the marinade:-
30 ml/2 tbsp olive oil
1 garlic clove, peeled and crushed
25 g/1 oz red onions, peeled and finely chopped
1 red chilli, deseeded and finely sliced
1 tsp chipotle chilli sauce (see Resources)
1 tbsp flat leaf parsley, finely chopped
1 tsp mint, finely chopped

4 lamb chops

For the lentils:-
60 ml/4 tbsp olive oil
200 g/7 oz onions, peeled and coarsely chopped
1 garlic clove, peeled and crushed
1 red chilli, deseeded and sliced
1 tsp cumin seeds, coarsely ground in a mortar or spice grinder
200 g/7 oz red lentils, rinsed under cold running water
500 ml/17 fl oz water
1 tsp bouillon powder
1 tbsp chipotle chilli sauce (see Resources)
15 g/½ oz flat leaf parsley, coarsely chopped

15 g/½ oz mint, coarsely chopped
Sea salt and freshly ground black pepper

Mix all the ingredients for the marinade in an ovenproof china dish. Add the lamb chops and spoon the marinade over them so that they are well coated. Set aside for at least 2 hours, turning them over every now and then.

Heat 2 tbsp of olive oil in a saucepan and add the onions, garlic and chilli. Cook over medium heat for 5 minutes until softened. Sprinkle in the cumin and cook, stirring, for a further minute. Add the lentils, water, bouillon powder and chilli sauce. Bring to the boil, cover the pan and simmer very gently for 30 minutes. Stir in 2 tbsp of the olive oil and season to taste.

About 15 minutes before the lentils are ready, heat the grill to high. Baste the lamb chops with the marinade and grill them, still in their china dish, about 10 cm/4 in from the heat for 5 minutes on each side if you like them pink, or 7 minutes if you prefer them well done.

Place the lentils on two warmed plates, top with the lamb chops and any juices in the dish and sprinkle with herbs.

Serve immediately.

YUCATECAN LAMB STEW
Estofado Yucateco

This is as close as I have been able to get to a dish which we ate at a lakeside restaurant near the Mayan ruins of Cobá. The cook stood behind a magnificent buffet set out on a long table covered with banana leaves, and was proud to describe his Yucatecan cuisine to me. He used both the milk and grated flesh of fresh coconuts in his *estofado,* but having found this a tad impractical, I have opted for tinned coconut milk which does not give quite the same result – but as I say, it is close enough! The coconut is actually barely discernible – it just imparts a faint, tropical sweetness which blends with the raisiny flavour of the *pasilla* chillies and keeps the aggressive *habañeros* in their place.

Serves 4

30 g/1 ¼ oz pasilla chillies (see Resources)
120 ml/4 fl oz water
60 ml/4 tbsp olive oil
4 large lamb leg steaks, about 200 g/7 oz each, or lamb shanks
250 g/9 oz onions, peeled and coarsely chopped
2 garlic cloves, peeled and crushed
1 tbsp ground cinnamon
5 whole cloves
1 x quantity Roasted Tomatoes (page 205), puréed in a food processor
2 habañero chillies, dried or fresh (see Resources)
1 tbsp bouillon powder
50 g/2 oz raisins
1 x 400 g/14 oz tin coconut milk
15 g/½ oz fresh coriander, coarsely chopped
Sea salt and freshly ground black pepper

Heat a heavy frying pan over medium heat and toast the chillies, pressing down on them with a spatula, until they start to smell aromatic, about 3 minutes. Flip them over and do the same on the other side. Place them in a bowl, cover with boiling water, put a small saucepan lid or plate on top to keep them submerged, and set them aside to soak for 30 minutes. Drain them and discard the stems, seeds and ribs. Place them in a food processor with the water and process until smooth. Strain the purée through a medium mesh sieve to remove any bits of skin.

While the chillies are soaking, heat 2 tbsp of olive oil in a large frying pan or casserole and brown the lamb well all over. Remove to a plate and add the remaining 2 tbsp of olive oil, the onions and the garlic to the pan. Cook, stirring occasionally, for about 15 minutes, until soft and golden. Add the spices and stir-fry for a couple of minutes, then add the tomatoes, chilli purée, habañero chillies, bouillon powder, raisins and some seasoning. Simmer for 10 minutes, until thickened. Stir in the coconut milk, add the lamb, cover the pan and leave to cook over very low heat for about 2 hours, until the lamb is meltingly tender and you have a thick, rich, brick-coloured sauce. Give it a stir every now and then to make sure it is not sticking to the bottom.

Fish out the habañero chillies and discard them. Check the seasoning and sprinkle with coriander.

Serve immediately.

Alternatively, this stew keeps well and the flavour benefits from maturing for a couple of days in the refrigerator. Reheat very gently before serving.

SAUSAGES AND MASH
Salchichas con Anchos y Puré de Frijol

Mexican sausages are rich, zesty and utterly delectable, always spiked with a bit of chilli, and on occasions far too hot for me. Herby sausages work well in this recipe – rosemary and honey for instance, or sage and onion. *Ancho* chillies are dried *poblanos*, gently spicy rather than fiery, reminiscent of dried fruit and herb honey. This is an earthy, rustic dish, which sticks to your ribs, perfect after a long winter walk or on a chilly night in front of the fire.

Serves 2

25 g/1 oz ancho chillies (see Resources)
½ x quantity Roasted Tomatoes (page 205)
1 tbsp olive oil
100 g/4 oz onions, peeled and coarsely chopped
2 garlic cloves, peeled and crushed
120 ml/4 fl oz water
8 sausages
½ x quantity Bean Mash (page 24)
Sea salt and freshly ground black pepper

Heat a heavy frying pan over medium heat and toast the chillies, pressing down on them with a spatula, until they start to smell aromatic, about 3 minutes. Flip them over and do the same on the other side. Place them in a bowl, cover with boiling water, put a small saucepan lid or plate on top to keep them submerged, and set them aside to soak for 30 minutes. Drain, discard the stems, seeds and ribs, and place in a food processor. Add the roasted tomatoes and process until fairly smooth.

Heat the olive oil in a frying pan, add the onions and garlic and cook until soft and golden. Add the tomato and chilli purée and cook gently for 10 minutes, until thickened. Stir in the water and some seasoning.

Cook the sausages in a frying pan until crusty and brown. Pour the sauce on top of them and stir to coat the sausages. Bring to the boil and simmer for 10 minutes. Check the seasoning.

While the sausages are cooking, place the bean mash in a heavy-bottomed saucepan and reheat it over very low heat, stirring often. Add a bit of water if it is very stiff.

Place the mash on two warm plates, top with the sausages and sauce and serve immediately.

PORK CHOPS IN CHILLI MARINADE
Chuletas Adobadas

Anything *adobado* has been slathered with a gutsy chilli paste and left to marinate for hours, until the flavours blend and meld and permeate the whole dish. Dried chillies are always used and they can be varied according to taste and courage. For this simple recipe, I have used *pasillas* as I love their caramel fruitiness with pork. The chops get a slow, lengthy cook and come out of the oven tender enough to eat with a spoon.

Serves 4

For the marinade:-
25 g/1 oz pasilla chillies (see Resources)
100 ml/3 ½ fl oz water
½ tsp ground cloves
1 tsp Mexican oregano (see Resources)
1 tsp cumin seeds, coarsely ground in a mortar or spice grinder
1 tbsp cider or wine vinegar
1 tbsp olive oil
1 tsp sea salt
1 tsp soft brown sugar
50 g/2 oz onions, peeled and coarsely chopped
2 garlic cloves, peeled

4 large pork chops, about 250 g/9 oz each
1 x quantity Grilled Tomato Sauce (page 204)

Heat a heavy frying pan over medium heat and toast the chillies, pressing down on them with a spatula, until they start to smell aromatic, about 3 minutes. Flip them over and do the same on the other side. Place them in a bowl, cover with boiling water, put a small saucepan lid or plate on top to keep them submerged, and set them aside to soak for 30 minutes. Drain, discard the stems, seeds and ribs, and process in a food processor with the water and all the other marinade ingredients until you have a fairly smooth purée. Add a bit more water if necessary.

Place the pork chops in a china or glass baking dish and coat them well with the chilli paste. Leave them to marinate for as long as possible, at least half an hour.

Heat the oven to 180°C/350°F/gas 4/fan oven 160°C. Wrap the baking dish in a double layer of kitchen foil and bake the chops for 2 hours.

Turn the oven off. Remove the foil and transfer the chops to a warm serving dish with a spatula; put them back in the oven, leaving the oven door ajar.

Heat the tomato sauce in a saucepan and add all the cooking juices and chilli paste from the baking dish. Bring to the boil and check the seasoning; add a bit more sugar if the sauce is too sharp.

Spoon some sauce over the chops and serve immediately with the remaining sauce on the side.

CHILLI, POTATO AND SAUSAGE HASH
Papas con Rajas y Salchichas

These wonderfully savoury and spicy potatoes were part of the breakfast buffet at a lovely old colonial *hacienda* near the ruins of Uxmal where we ate in a sunny central patio garden full of flowering oleanders. The dish struck me immediately as being very Spanish, reminiscent of the Andalucian *Patatas del Pobre* – but it is of course the other way around, as potatoes and chillies came to Spain from the Americas. However, the addition of the porky bits is decidedly Spanish. A Mexican cook would fry everything up together in one large pan, but roasting the potatoes gives them a lovely crunchy exterior, requires less attention, and produces a lighter dish.

Serves 4

1 kg/2 ¼ lb potatoes, scrubbed and cut into 2 cm/¾ in pieces
60 ml/4 tbsp olive oil
100 g/4 oz chorizo sausage, diced
8 sausages
1 x quantity Multicoloured Rajas (page 103)
Sea salt and freshly ground black pepper

Heat the oven to 200°C/400°F/gas 6/fan oven 180°C.

Bring a large pot of salted water to the boil and cook the potatoes for 5 minutes. Drain well, cover the pan with a lid and give it all a good shake to rough up the edges of the potatoes a bit. Transfer them to a roasting tin, drizzle with olive oil, season well, and roast, stirring occasionally, until brown and crisp, about one hour.

While the potatoes are roasting, cook the chorizo in a heavy dry frying pan over medium heat, stirring often, until it has released most of its fat and is golden, about 10 minutes. With a slotted spoon, remove it to a plate lined with kitchen paper to drain. Add the sausages to the frying pan and cook them as slowly as possible, turning them every now and then, until golden.

When everything is ready, stir the chorizo and rajas into the potatoes and return it all to the oven for 5 minutes to reheat. Arrange the sausages on top and serve immediately.

GRATIN OF POTATOES, PEPPERS AND *CHORIZO*
Papas con Rajas y Chorizo

Rich and mellow, but well spiked with the heat of the *poblanos* and chillies, this delicious gratin is almost a meal in itself and makes a wonderful supper dish with a salad. If you don't like too much heat, leave the chillies out, as the *poblanos* are enough to give the dish some oomph – but if you have been unable to find *poblanos* and have used green peppers in the *rajas*, you will need to include at least one mild green chilli. I tend to use the multicoloured *rajas* because their faint sweetness goes so well with the spicy, savoury chorizo.

Serves 4

100 g/4 oz chorizo sausage, the spicier the better, diced
700 g/1 ½ lb potatoes, scrubbed and finely sliced
2 hot green chillies, deseeded and cut into long thin strips
1 x quantity Multicoloured Rajas (page 103)
250 ml/8 fl oz double cream
Sea salt and freshly ground black pepper
1 x 1.5 litres/2 ½ pints baking dish

Cook the chorizo in a heavy, dry frying pan over medium heat until it has released most of its fat and is golden, about 10 minutes. With a slotted spoon, remove it to a plate lined with kitchen paper to drain.

Spread half the potato slices over the bottom of the baking dish and season. Stir the chillies and chorizo into the *rajas,* and spread them over the potatoes. Arrange the remaining potatoes on top – in an overlapping pattern if you have the time and can be bothered! – and season again. Pour the cream over everything.

Heat the oven to 200°C / 400°F / gas 6 / fan oven 180°C and bake the gratin until the potatoes are cooked and golden, about one hour – test for doneness with the tip of a knife and if they feel a bit hard still, cover the dish with foil and cook for a further 20 minutes before testing again. You are looking for a soft, unctuous texture.

Leave the gratin to rest for 10 minutes before serving.

CAULIFLOWER IN *ADOBO* SAUCE
Coliflor en Adobo

The young waiter in a restaurant in Mérida kept hovering and when he finally caught my eye, he pointed out to me in a low voice that the cauliflower had *habañeros* in it. We had chosen the set menu and therefore did not know what we were being served, but I was deeply grateful to him for mentioning to me that the cauliflower was likely to damage my palate for life! With 10/10 on the heat scale, *hubañeros* are widely used in the Yucatán and are not to be trifled with. Luckily their lantern shape is easy to spot and they can be fished out and discarded before serious injury is inflicted.

Serves 4

30 g/1 ¼ oz whole blanched almonds
Olive oil
1 medium cauliflower, broken into florets
150 g/5 oz onions, peeled and sliced
1 tbsp cumin seeds, coarsely ground in a mortar or spice grinder
500 g/18 oz tomatoes, skinned and coarsely chopped
20 g/¾ oz raisins
2 habañero chillies, fresh or dried (see Resources)
15 g/½ oz fresh coriander, coarsely chopped
Sea salt and freshly ground black pepper

Heat the oven to 150°C/300°F/gas 2/fan oven 135°C. Place the almonds on a baking tray and cook in the oven for about 10 minutes, until lightly browned. Cool and chop coarsely.

Cauliflower, like aubergine, tends to absorb as much oil as you are willing to give it, so start off by heating just 2 tbsp in a large, heavy frying pan. Add the florets and cook, turning occasionally, until they are patched with gold. If the pan gets very dry, pour in a bit more olive oil. Remove the cauliflower to a plate and set aside.

Add 2 tbsp of olive oil to the frying pan, stir in the onions and cook over medium heat until soft and translucent. Sprinkle in the cumin and stir-fry for a minute, then add the tomatoes, raisins, chillies and some seasoning. Turn the heat down and cook gently for 10 minutes, until the tomatoes have broken down and the sauce has thickened. Stir in the cauliflower, coating the florets well with the sauce, cover the frying pan and leave to simmer for 15 minutes, stirring occasionally, until the cauliflower is tender.

Check the seasoning and fish out the chillies – or leave them in if you dare. Stir in the almonds, transfer to a warm serving dish and sprinkle with coriander.

Serve immediately.

SWEET POTATO PURÉE

Puré de Camote

Sweet potatoes roasted in hot coals are one of the many delights offered by street vendors and market stalls. They are smoky-tasting, and sharp from the fresh lime juice squeezed over the flesh when the skin is sliced open. Soured cream is often also offered, as is a strong spicy *salsa*. This purée is a more sophisticated version which we found in a restaurant in Mexico City, served with a simple grilled chicken breast which had been marinated in chilli and lime – a delicious combination.

The purée can be prepared ahead of time and reheated in a bowl over a pan of simmering water.

Serves 4

900 g/2 lb sweet potatoes, scrubbed
1 lime, juiced
1 tsp chipotle chilli sauce (see Resources)
60 ml/4 tbsp olive oil
100 ml/3 ½ fl oz soured cream or Greek-style plain yoghurt
1 red chilli and 1 green chilli, deseeded and chopped
15 g/½ oz fresh coriander, coarsely chopped
Sea salt and freshly ground black pepper

Heat the oven to 200°C/400°F/gas 6/fan oven 180°C and bake the potatoes, in their skins, for about one hour, until they are soft when squeezed. Cool them slightly, cut them in half and scoop the flesh into a food processor. Add the lime juice, chilli sauce, olive oil and some salt and pepper, and process until smooth. Check the spiciness and add a bit more chilli sauce if the flavour is a bit too sweet or flat – it all depends on the sugar content of the potatoes.

Scrape the purée into a warm serving dish, drizzle the soured cream or yoghurt over it, and sprinkle with the chopped chillies and coriander.

Serve immediately.

La serpiente emplumada

stone

Misión Jesuita, Satevo

The Spaniards called it the 'pear of the Indies', preferring not to use its local name – for reasons which I shall explain later. Its skin is smooth and glossy, or dark, rugged and craggy like an alligator. Its flesh is rich, luscious and deeply nourishing. And in its centre lies a large, egg-shaped stone, a jewel nestling in its soft, buttery heart. Discard this stone and the fruit turns dull and brown as though its life supply has been switched off; but add it to your *guacamole*, soup, *salsa* or salad, and the gentle, faintly luminous green will glow for hours. The stone also heralds over-ripeness: shake the 'pear' and if you hear a tell-tale rattle from its stone, reject it as it is past its prime and the inside will be dark and vaguely musty. In the northern states, the stone is dried and grated into *enchilada* sauce to provide an unusual hint of bitterness – very much an acquired taste.

The *ahuacatl* was first cultivated in Mexico, probably around 500BC. It was a forbidden fruit for the Aztecs, who deemed it to be a sexual stimulant, but other Mexican cultures had no such hesitation and ate it straight from its shell, scraping the soft flesh out with their front teeth. The name actually means testicle in *Nahuatl* which perhaps explains why no *ahuacacuauhitl* – 'testicle trees' – were ever planted in the gardens of the Spanish missions. Luckily this did not stop the avocado from becoming an essential ingredient in Mexican cooking and Hernán Cortés came to enjoy avocadoes, sprinkling them with salt and eating them somewhat more elegantly than the local population, with a small silver spoon. In its natural state, its flavour is faintly nutty, decidedly delicate and elusive, but give it a partner like lime juice or tomato, onions or garlic, fresh coriander or salty cheese, and it undergoes a magical transformation – no longer timid and hesitant, it spins and sparkles, lending its talents to any number of happy combinations.

Avocado leaves are also extensively used in Mexico, lightly toasted over a naked flame or in a dry frying pan to bring out their gentle aniseed flavour and then crumbled. Unfortunately fresh ones are not widely available outside Mexico – and fortunately they are not an essential ingredient! Dried avocado leaves can be purchased by mail order if you fancy experimenting with them.

Guacamole's fame has spread far and wide, to the extent that you can buy it in a tub nowadays, and even a 'long-life' version in a jar. But avocadoes only shine when they are freshly extracted from their knobbly skins. Their allure, like their colour, fades rapidly when exposed to oxygen and their frailty is soon laid bare as more robust flavours intensify and take control. Nevertheless, sometimes it is their texture which makes the greatest contribution, so if you decide to take the *tortas* (page 173) on a picnic, the avocado may not be a vivid green but its richness will still be a perfect foil for the spicy beans and roast chicken.

Avocadoes also work well in sweet dishes, which is not surprising bearing in mind that they are a fruit rather than a vegetable. In a fruit salad, for instance, their rich smoothness contrasts very successfully with acid tropical fruit like pineapple, papaya and mango. I am not a fan of avocado icecream – an interesting experience at best – but an avocado *licuado*, or smoothie, is a delicious energy booster, packed with fibre, unsaturated fat, vitamins and minerals. Wonderful fresh fruit juices and smoothies are found all over Mexico in *juguerías* – juice bars, where you can order anything from a straightforward orange juice to the most exotic combinations. I tried numerous avocado concoctions and loved them, particularly when sweet spices or nuts were included.

GUACAMOLE

Everybody makes *guacamole* their own way. If you want to be traditional, by all means pound it in a mortar. I usually make it in a food processor because it is quicker than chopping onions and coriander or crushing garlic. If more texture is required, mash it with a fork. Sometimes I leave the tomatoes and chillies out, depending on what I am using it for – if it is acting as a sauce, as in the Yucatecan Marinated Salmon (page 180), I prefer it simple and smooth; if it is going to sit on a hotcake (page 87), then I want it chunkier and spicier. Always remember to put the stone back in to keep it from discolouring. The *guacamole* will last for about 2 hours but any longer than that and it will lose freshness and sparkle.

Serves 4

2 large, ripe avocadoes
2 garlic cloves, peeled
1 green chilli, deseeded and coarsely chopped
100 g/4 oz red onions, peeled and coarsely chopped
1 lime, juiced
60 ml/4 tbsp olive oil
15 g/½ oz fresh coriander plus a few leaves for garnish
150 g/5 oz cherry tomatoes, quartered – a mixture of red and yellow is pretty
Tortilla chips (optional)
Sea salt and freshly ground black pepper

Halve the avocadoes and set the stones aside. Scoop the flesh into the bowl of a food processor with the garlic, chilli, onions, half the lime juice, olive oil, 15 g/½ oz of coriander and some seasoning. Process until smooth. Scrape into a bowl, fold in the tomatoes and push the avocado stones into the guacamole.

Just before serving, remove the stones, stir gently, and check the seasoning – if it is not sharp enough, add a bit more lime juice.

Garnish with the fresh coriander leaves and serve immediately, with *totopos*, tortilla chips, as a snack or hors d'oeuvre.

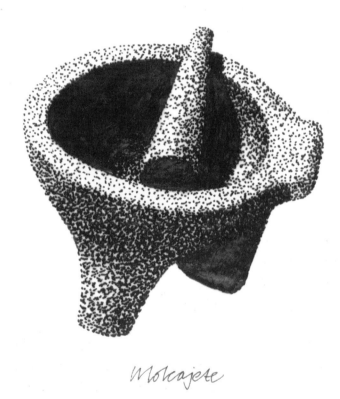

Molcajete

AVOCADO SALAD
Ensalada de Aguacate

This salad is infinitely versatile and we came across countless version of it – with roasted *poblano* chillies, fruit, peanuts, coconut, different cheeses, and pumpkin seed or avocado oil instead of olive oil which takes it to a whole new level – including expense! It is fresh and energising somehow, with wonderful contrasts of texture and flavour, rich and creamy, sharp and crunchy, hot and sweet. Although I am suggesting a "fan" of avocado slices because it looks pretty, it is a rather *nouvelle cuisine* presentation and the market cooks simply spoon the avocado out of its shell. Suit yourself!

Serves 4

20 g/¾ oz hulled pumpkin seeds
1 tsp + 2 tbsp/30 ml olive oil
2 small ripe avocadoes
225 g/8 oz cherry tomatoes, quartered
30 g/1 ¼ oz red onions, peeled and finely sliced
1 lime, juiced
1 red or green chilli, deseeded and finely sliced
100 g/4 oz Feta cheese, crumbled
15 g/½ oz flat leaf parsley, coarsely chopped
Sea salt and freshly ground black pepper

Heat the oven to 180°C/350°F/gas 4/fan oven 160°C. Place the pumpkin seeds in a small baking dish and stir in 1 tsp of olive oil and ¼ tsp of salt. Roast for about 7 minutes, until the seeds are slightly swollen and barely starting to brown. Set aside to cool.

Halve and stone the avocadoes, and peel off the skin with a sharp knife. Lay the halves on a chopping board hollow side down and slice through them 4 or 5 times at an angle, leaving them attached at the narrow end. With the palm of your hand, flatten each half gently so that the slices fan out. Slide a spatula under the fans and place them on four plates. Top with the tomatoes and then the onions. Season and drizzle with lime juice and the remaining olive oil. Sprinkle with chilli, then cheese and parsley, and finally the roasted pumpkin seeds.

Serve immediately before the avocado loses its colour.

AVOCADO SALSA
Salsa de Aguacate

Queso fresco, 'fresh cheese', is widely used in Mexico and sold in huge white blocks in the markets. The stallholders hack off pieces to order with a large, heavy knife and wrap it in waxed paper for the housewives to carry home in their baskets. It is firm, quite salty, and tangy, rather like a fresh goat's cheese. Feta is the best substitute, because it crumbles easily, although its flavour is somewhat stronger.

This *salsa* is truly multi-talented and its uses only limited by one's imagination. Apart from the recipes in this chapter, it can be served on its own with tortilla chips, as an hors d'oeuvre with drinks, a first course or a light lunch; on toast, in a baked potato, as a salad dressing or spooned through roasted vegetables, as a garnish for a steak – the possibilities are literally endless.

125 g/4 ½ oz red cherry tomatoes, quartered
50 g/2 oz red onions, finely chopped
1 garlic clove, peeled and crushed
1 red chilli, deseeded and finely sliced
30 ml/2 tbsp olive oil
2 small ripe avocadoes
15 g/½ oz fresh coriander, coarsely chopped
30 ml/2 tbsp fresh lime juice, about 1 large lime
100 g/4 oz Feta cheese
Sea salt and freshly ground black pepper

Place the tomatoes, onions, garlic, chilli and olive oil in a bowl, season and mix gently.

Peel and stone the avocadoes and dice into 1cm/½ in pieces. Add to the bowl with the coriander and lime juice. Crumble over the Feta cheese and stir it all together gently. Add the avocado stones if you are not going to eat the salsa immediately – and remember to remove them!

The salsa may be prepared up to half an hour beforehand but after that, the avocado starts to discolour and its stone will be powerless to protect it.

FISH MARINATED IN LIME JUICE
Seviche

Seviche is forever associated in my mind with holidays in Acapulco, the big, glitzy beach resort on the Pacific coast where we spent our Christmas holidays. Every restaurant served this "seafood cocktail". The raw fish is marinated in fresh lime juice for several hours and the acid in effect cooks the fish. It is wonderfully clean-tasting, sharp, zesty and aromatic. However, it is essential to use absolutely fresh fish so buy it from a reliable fishmonger.

As far as I remember, the *seviche* was invariably served as a stuffing in the hollow of the avocado – very sixties and seventies! – but I prefer an avocado "fan" – dreadfully *nouvelle cuisine*, I know, but it does look pretty and it is easier to eat.

I tend to use monkfish because of its firm texture, which makes it easy to slice thinly, but salmon works well, as do scallops which are better diced than sliced.

Serves 2

175 g/6 oz monkfish fillet, skinned
2 limes, juiced
100 g/4 oz tomatoes, skinned and coarsely chopped
30 ml/2 tbsp olive oil
1 garlic clove, peeled
20 g/¾ oz red onions, peeled and finely chopped
1 orange, peeled and segmented, juice reserved
1 green and 1 red chilli, deseeded and finely sliced
1 tsp runny honey
15 g/½ oz mint, coarsely chopped
1 ripe avocado
2 lime wedges
Sea salt and freshly ground black pepper

Slice the monkfish very thinly and place it in a glass or china bowl. Stir in the lime juice, cover with clingfilm and leave to marinate in the refrigerator for 24 hours, giving it a stir whenever you remember.

Put the tomatoes, olive oil, garlic and some seasoning in a food processor, and process to a smooth purée. Scrape into a bowl and add the onions, orange and any reserved orange juice, chillies and honey.

Drain the seviche well in a colander and add it to the tomato purée.

Halve and stone the avocado, and peel off the skin with a sharp knife. Lay the halves hollow side down on a chopping board and slice through them 4 or 5 times at an angle, leaving them attached at the narrow end. With the palm of your hand, flatten each half gently so that the slices fan out. Slide a spatula under the fans and place them on two plates.

Spoon the seviche around and partially over the avocado, sprinkle with mint and serve immediately, with lime wedges to squeeze over everything.

AVOCADO, ORANGE AND MUSTARD SOUP

Sopa de Aguacate, Naranja y Mostaza

This is a light, fresh-tasting soup. It is vital not to overcook it as it loses both its greatest assets – its colour and its delicate flavour, so be careful in winter. However, it can luckily also be served cold. Proceed as below but cool the onion mixture completely before processing with the avocadoes, and once you have added all the stock and the orange juice and rind, chill the soup for an hour or so – the acidity of the orange will keep it from turning brown too quickly. Fresh orange segments and whole coriander leaves make a pretty and colourful garnish.

Serves 2

1 tbsp olive oil
100 g/4 oz onions, peeled and coarsely chopped
1 tsp cumin seeds, coarsely ground in a mortar or spice grinder
2 oranges
2 small ripe avocadoes
¼ tsp English mustard or to taste
500 ml/17 fl oz chicken or vegetable stock or water with ½ tsp bouillon powder
Fresh orange segments, to garnish (optional)
Fresh coriander leaves, to garnish (optional)
Sea salt and freshly ground black pepper

Heat the olive oil in a medium saucepan and cook the onions for about 10 minutes, until soft and translucent. Add the cumin and cook for 3 minutes longer. Cool slightly.

Grate the rind from the oranges and squeeze the juice into a small bowl.

Peel and stone the avocadoes, scoop the flesh out of the skin and place in a food processor. Add some seasoning, the mustard, half the stock and the onions. Process until smooth. Return to the saucepan, add the rest of the stock, the orange rind and juice and reheat carefully – do not allow the soup to boil or it will go khaki. Check the seasoning and add a bit more mustard if it needs more kick.

Serve immediately, garnished with orange segments and coriander leaves.

GAZPACHO
Caldo de Tomate Frío

I had always assumed that *gazpacho* was a typically Spanish dish, but having eaten this cold tomato soup on a number of occasions, and particularly in small, local restaurants, it occurred to me that its origins, and indeed most of its components, are probably far more New World than Old World.

A fairly hot chilli works well here as the milder ones tend to get lost in the brightness of the soup. The yoghurt is not typical but it contributes substantially to the texture, as does the goat's cheese which somehow melts into the soup as you eat it – but a hard crumbly cheese like Feta is used in Mexico.

Serves 2

500 g/18 oz tomatoes
1 garlic clove, peeled
30 ml/2 tbsp Greek-style plain yoghurt
30 ml/2 tbsp olive oil
½ tsp chipotle chilli sauce (see Resources)
1 small ripe avocado
20 g/¾ oz red onions, peeled and finely chopped
2 hot green chillies, deseeded and finely chopped
100 g/4 oz fresh goat's cheese, crumbled
Fresh coriander leaves
Sea salt and freshly ground black pepper

Process the tomatoes, garlic, yoghurt, olive oil, chipotle chilli sauce and some seasoning in a food processor until really smooth. Strain it through a medium mesh sieve into a bowl and refrigerate until you are ready to serve.

Peel, stone and dice the avocado into 1cm/½ in pieces. Mix the onions and chillies in a small bowl.

Check the soup for seasoning and ladle it into two soup plates. Sprinkle the avocado and goat's cheese over it and top with the onion and chilli mixture. Garnish with coriander leaves.

Serve immediately.

CONSOMMÉ WITH MEXICAN FLAVOURS
Consomé a la Mexicana

Wander around any Mexican market and you will be struck by the countless chickens on the butchers' counters. It is difficult to believe that there is a demand for quite so many of them! They are of course cheap compared to beef or lamb for instance, but even so... I remembered expeditions with our cook to San Juán market in Mexico City and revisited it with tremendous nostalgia. It is not a market as such, more a grid of streets lined with nothing but food shops, fresh fruit and vegetable barrows, and cooks' stands – the aroma of chillies, coriander and frying tomatoes follows you wherever you go and everyone seems to be eating something. In the butchers' shops, the marble counters are piled high with chickens, hundreds if not thousands of them; their bare plucked skin is bright yellow like the corn they eat, their heads dangle forlornly, their scaly feet stick out stiffly – and they are bursting with flavour, their flesh juicy, firm and rich. Chicken was an Old World addition to the New World diet and plays a major part in Mexican cookery, making its faithful appearance on every restaurant menu in many different guises, from a plain, steaming broth thickened with little pasta shapes, to a savoury soup full of vegetables and chicken strips, a filling for the many tortilla dishes, or dark, spicy *moles*. *Consomé* is a childhood favourite for me, a comforting, fragrant supper dish which I never tired of and which still has the power to soothe me and make me feel safe.

Serves 2

2 large chicken thighs or drumsticks
350 ml/12 fl oz chicken stock or water
1 tbsp olive oil
100 g/4 oz red onions, peeled and finely chopped
2 garlic cloves, peeled and crushed
1 red and 1 green chilli, deseeded and finely chopped
150 g/5 oz tomatoes, coarsely chopped
1 cup cooked brown rice
1 ripe avocado
20 g/¾ oz flat leaf parsley, coarsely chopped
Sea salt and freshly ground black pepper

Place the chicken and stock or water in a small saucepan. Bring to the boil on low heat and simmer for 10 minutes. Set aside to cool. Remove the chicken from the stock, discard the skin, and strip the meat from the bones. Reserve the stock.

Heat the olive oil in a medium saucepan. Add the onions, garlic, chillies and some seasoning, and cook gently until softened. Stir in the tomatoes and cook for about 5 minutes, to evaporate some of the moisture. Pour in the reserved chicken stock, stir in the rice and chicken, and bring to the boil.

Peel and stone the avocado, and dice the flesh into 1 cm / ½ in pieces. Add it to the soup and check the seasoning.

Stir in the parsley and serve immediately, before the avocado softens too much or loses its colour.

MY FAVOURITE *TORTA*

Carmen made *tortas* every morning for us to take to school as our mid-morning snack. The fillings varied, but this was by far my favourite the flavours of Mexico in a *telera*, a flattish Mexican roll. *Torterías* are found on virtually every street corner of every Mexican town, their long and wonderfully imaginative menus displayed on large boards, the cooks standing behind piles of bread rolls and bowls of fresh, aromatic ingredients, making the *tortas* to order for each customer.

You need a big bread roll for *tortas*, as they have to be well filled. I often use something called *grand rustique*, or a ciabatta loaf: discard the narrow ends, fill it all in one go and then slice it into four.

I have to admit that this particular *torta* takes time to make, but it is well worth the effort and a good way to use up left-over chicken and refried beans. And it is the best picnic food imaginable, so long as you wrap it very tightly in foil or clingfilm – the flavours and moisture all soak into the bread and if you take it on a long winter walk, when you sit down to eat it among the dry, crackling autumn leaves, it will bring a glow to your cheeks and warm every corner of your chilled body.

Serves 2/4

4 large crusty rolls
Butter, softened
½ x quantity cold Refried Beans (page 16)
1 large skinless, boneless chicken breast, cooked and shredded
½ x quantity Guacamole (page 159)
100 ml/3 ½ fl oz full fat crème fraîche
4 Cos lettuce leaves, finely sliced

Split the rolls and open them up. Butter both halves liberally and then layer the filling up on the bottom half, starting off with beans, then chicken, guacamole, cream and finally lettuce. Replace the top and press down gently. Eat immediately, or wrap the tortas tightly in clingfilm and refrigerate.

Make sure you have plenty of paper napkins to hand as eating these tortas can be a very messy business!

Torta

CHILAQUILES IN *TOMATILLO* SAUCE
Chilaquiles Verdes

Although *chilaquiles* have their roots firmly in peasant and poverty cooking, one comes across fancier, and often over-smartened, versions in restaurants, where the true essence of the dish is eclipsed by the 'costume jewelry'. However, we came across this particular combination on a number of occasions – and enjoyed its contrasts: sharp tomatillos, rich bacon, savoury cheese. I love to serve it Mexican style, for breakfast – perhaps brunch is more accurate – on a Sunday morning. It takes virtually no time to put together so long as you have some tomatillo sauce to hand – and since the sauce freezes perfectly, it is worth having a bag or two in the freezer just for these *chilaquiles*.

Serves 2

4 rashers smoked streaky bacon or pancetta, rinded
2 small ripe avocadoes
2 x quantities Cooked Tomatillo Sauce (page 206)
300 g/11 oz plain tortilla chips
100 g/4 oz Feta cheese
Sea salt and freshly ground black pepper

Heat the grill to high. Line the grill pan with foil, place the bacon or pancetta on it and grill until crisp. Remove to a plate lined with kitchen paper to drain. Cool slightly and crumble.

Peel the avocadoes and dice the flesh into 1 cm / ½ in pieces.

Bring the tomatillo sauce to the boil in a large frying pan and add the tortilla chips. Turn them over and over in the sauce with a large spoon until they are well coated and start to soften.

Divide the chilaquiles between two warm plates, top with the avocado and bacon, crumble the Feta cheese over everything and serve immediately.

PASTA WITH AVOCADO SALSA AND SMOKED SALMON
Espaguetis con Salsa de Aguacate y Salmón Ahumado

A Mexican cook would use smoked tuna or swordfish – but, apart from the fact that smoked salmon is cheaper and more easily available, pink salmon and green avocado is a picture perfect colour combination! This is a decidedly modern dish, almost *nouvelle cuisine* or *haute cuisine* – *alta cocina* – and therefore rather middle-class, so it is unlikely that you will find it at a street stand, but the ingredients are very traditional and typical of Mexican cooking.

This is an ideal summer dish, as the sauce does not require any cooking, and you can almost (but not quite!) throw it together while the spaghetti is cooking. But don't hesitate to make it in winter, as the flavours are rich and satisfying enough to blot out the coldest night.

Serves 4

125 g/4 ½ oz red cherry tomatoes, quartered
50 g/2 oz red onions, finely chopped
1 garlic clove, peeled and crushed
1 red chilli, deseeded and finely sliced
30 ml/2 tbsp olive oil
2 small ripe avocadoes
15 g/½ oz fresh coriander, coarsely chopped
30 ml/2 tbsp fresh lime juice, about 1 large lime
150 g/5 oz smoked salmon, cut into strips
100 g/4 oz Feta cheese
750 g/1 ¾ lb spaghetti or other thin pasta
Sea salt and freshly ground black pepper

Place the tomatoes, onions, garlic, chilli and olive oil in a bowl, season and mix. Peel and stone the avocadoes and dice the flesh into 1 cm / ½ in pieces. Add to the bowl with the coriander, lime juice and smoked salmon. Crumble over the Feta cheese and stir it all together gently.

Cook the pasta in boiling salted water according to the manufacturer's instructions. Drain well, place in four warm bowls, and top with the salsa.

Serve immediately.

RAJAS OMELETTE WITH *SALSA* AND AVOCADO FILLING
Omelet de Rajas y Aguacate

The perfect way to start a lazy Sunday! To make it into a real Mexican breakfast – *desayuno* – begin with a freshly squeezed juice like pink grapefruit, then a plate of sliced, brilliantly coloured tropical fruit, followed by this savoury, nourishing omelette, and finish with a cup of hot chocolate. If you cook the peppers and onions the day before, the whole dish takes little time to prepare – or alternatively they could be cooking while you prepare the fruit. If you can't find a *poblano* chilli, a green pepper will be fine, as there is enough heat from the chillies in the *salsa*.

Serves 2

1 tbsp olive oil
1 medium poblano chilli (see Resources) or green pepper, about 150 g/5 oz, cut into 2 cm/¾ in wide strips
100 g/4 oz red onions, peeled and finely sliced
15 g/½ oz butter
6 large eggs
1 small ripe avocado
½ quantity Raw Tomato Salsa (page 201)
Sea salt and freshly ground black pepper

Heat the olive oil in a medium omelette pan or non-stick frying pan, and fry the poblano chilli or pepper and onions over medium heat, stirring occasionally, until soft and just starting to brown, about 15 minutes. Scrape them on to a plate and cool slightly.

Beat the eggs in a small bowl and add some seasoning. Return the omelette pan to the heat and add the butter, swirling it around as it melts to coat the pan well. When it is foaming, pour the eggs into the pan and stir them around gently for a couple of minutes, until they start to set on the bottom. Spread the chilli and onion mixture over the top, letting it sink down into the eggs. Turn the heat down to low and continue to cook the omelette undisturbed for about 3 minutes, until the bottom is set and golden and the top is soft and just a tiny bit runny.

While the omelette is cooking, peel the avocado and dice the flesh into 1cm/½ in pieces. Stir into the salsa.

When the omelette is ready, spoon about half the salsa into the middle, fold the top of the omelette over it with a palette knife, cut the omelette in half and slide each half on to a warm plate.

Serve immediately with the rest of the salsa on the side.

YUCATECAN MARINATED SALMON WITH *GUACAMOLE*

Tuna, swordfish, even cod would work well here, but I love using salmon because the colour combination is so pretty. The marinade is fragrant with the warm, tropical flavours and scents of the Yucatán and traditionally calls for an *habañero* chilli – use one if you dare! It is important not to let the fish sit in the marinade for longer than an hour, as the acidity in the orange and lime start to "cook" the fish and toughen the flesh. Plain cooked rice is a nice accompaniment, or the Plain Rice with Plantains on page 250, as the sweetness of the plantains fits well with the citrus and spice of the marinade.

Serves 4

For the marinade:-
1 tsp cumin seeds, coarsely ground in a mortar or spice grinder
1 tsp Mexican dried oregano (see Resources)
Good pinch of cayenne pepper
½ tsp ground cinnamon
Juice and grated rind of 1 orange
Juice and grated rind of 1 lime
30 ml/2 tbsp olive oil
1 red and 1 green chilli, deseeded and sliced

4 salmon fillets, about 175 g/6 oz each
15 g/½ oz fresh coriander, coarsely chopped
1 lime, quartered
1 x quantity Guacamole (page 159), without tomatoes or chillies
Sea salt and freshly ground black pepper

Whisk the marinade ingredients in a small bowl. Place the salmon fillets in a china or glass baking dish and pour the marinade over them. Set aside for an hour, turning the fillets halfway through.

Heat the oven to 200°C/400°F/gas 6/fan oven 180°C and bake the salmon, still in its dish, for 10 minutes, basting it with the marinade after 5 minutes.

Remove the salmon to four warm plates, pour any juices over the top, sprinkle with coriander and garnish with the lime wedges.

Serve immediately with the guacamole.

RED SNAPPER IN CORIANDER
Huachinango en Cilantro

Fresh coriander has always been by far my favourite herb – the scent always takes me straight back to the kitchen of my childhood or, more recently, to holidays full of light, sunshine, colour, and bold, spicy food. The flavours in this dish are wonderfully simple and pure: lime, fish and coriander. The topping is aromatic, crisp and crunchy while the sauce – a guacamole heavily laced with coriander – is smooth, rich and sharp. Any fish fillet – tuna, swordfish, salmon, cod – works well but red snapper is so very, very Mexican. We ate this dish in the market in Mérida, where the cook, with her beautifully sculpted and impassive Mayan face, fried the fish and breadcrumbs separately on her two-burner gas stove, and then assembled it all just before serving. I prefer to bake it all together – easier and lighter.

Serves 4

For the topping:-
Grated rind of 2 limes
100 g/4 oz wholemeal bread, weighed without crusts and torn into pieces
2 garlic cloves, peeled and coarsely chopped
40 g/1 ½ oz fresh coriander
10 ml/2 tsp olive oil

4 red snapper fillets, about 175 g/6 oz each
1 lime, juiced
15 ml/1 tbsp olive oil
Sea salt and freshly ground black pepper

For the sauce:-
2 large ripe avocadoes
1 garlic clove, peeled
2 spring onions, trimmed and coarsely chopped
1 lime, juiced
30 ml/2 tbsp olive oil

30 ml/2 tbsp water
65g/2 ½ oz fresh coriander, coarsely chopped
Sea salt and freshly ground black pepper

To make the topping, place all the ingredients in a food processor and process to fine crumbs.

Heat the oven to 200°C/400°F/gas 6/fan oven 180°C. Place the fish, skin side up, in a roasting tray, sprinkle with the lime juice and olive oil and season well. Strew the breadcrumb mixture over the top. Bake in the oven for 10 minutes until the fish is firm and the breadcrumbs crisp and just starting to brown.

While the fish is cooking, place all the ingredients for the sauce in a food processor and process until fairly smooth. Check the seasoning.

With a wide spatula, carefully transfer the fish fillets to four warm plates.

Serve immediately with the avocado sauce.

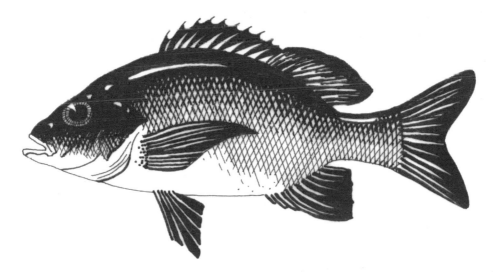

Huachinango

MEXICAN STIR-FRIED CHICKEN
Pollo a la Mexicana

This is a quick and easy dish to prepare, typical of market and street stall cooking, and full of bright, zappy flavours and contrasting textures. We came across several versions, with *poblano* chilli strips, different local cheeses or cooked beans, even carrot sticks or peas. The timing is fairly crucial as the dish loses its charm if it is over-cooked, so aim for good and warm rather than boiling hot. And eat it promptly before the *salsa* goes watery and the tortilla chips limp.

Serves 2

2 skinless, boneless chicken breasts
1 tsp cumin seeds, coarsely ground in a mortar or spice grinder
75 ml/5 tbsp olive oil
1 large ripe avocado
1 tbsp fresh lemon juice, about ½ large lemon
1 x quantity Raw Tomato Salsa (page 201)
50 g/2 oz tortilla chips
100 g/4 oz Feta cheese
15 g/½ oz fresh coriander leaves
Sea salt and freshly ground black pepper

Slice the chicken into strips the size of your little finger and place them in a bowl with the cumin and 2 tbsp of olive oil. Mix well and set aside.

Peel the avocado, dice the flesh into 1 cm / ½ in pieces and toss with the lemon juice.

Heat the remaining 3 tbsp of olive oil in a large frying pan or wok, add the chicken strips and stir-fry over high heat until firm and just starting to brown in places. Turn the heat down to low and add the salsa and tortilla chips, stirring for a minute or two, just to warm it all up – on no account bring it to the boil as the salsa will lose its freshness. Remove from the heat, add the avocado, crumble over the Feta cheese, and scatter with the coriander leaves.

Serve without delay.

ROAST CHICKEN WITH AVOCADO AND MANGO *SALSA*
Pollo al Horno con Salsa de Aguacate y Mango

Oaxaca is famous for its gastronomy, particularly its seven *moles*, but we were bitterly disappointed in its restaurants at first. It was only when we moved away from the touristy centre and down the side streets and alleyways that we were able to do some serious eating. We were served this *salsa* at a lovely courtyard restaurant full of Mexican families in their Sunday best. It was a little hors d'oeuvre and came with a bowl of *totopos*, tortilla chips; we finished it off with our main course of a simple roast chicken rubbed with cumin and oregano – a perfect partnership.

Serves 4

For the salsa:-
1 tsp cumin seeds
1 garlic clove, finely chopped
20 g/¾ oz red onions, finely chopped
1 small ripe mango, peeled and diced
1 small ripe avocado, peeled and diced
1 red chilli, deseeded and finely sliced
30 ml/2 tbsp olive oil
15 g/½ oz fresh coriander, coarsely chopped
1 lime, juiced – keep the halves to put in the chicken
Sea salt and freshly ground black pepper

1 tbsp cumin seeds, ground medium fine in a mortar or spice grinder
1 heaped tsp dried Mexican oregano (see Resources)
1 chicken, about 1.5 kg/3 lb
15 ml/1 tbsp olive oil
Sea salt and freshly ground black pepper

For the salsa, toast the cumin seeds in a heavy frying pan over medium heat, stirring all the time, until they release their aroma – 2 to 3 minutes – watch them carefully as they burn easily. Tip them into a mortar, add the oregano and grind it all with a pestle until medium fine – you want to keep a bit of texture. You can also do this in a spice grinder but avoid ending up with powder. If you can't be bothered with any of this, just use 1 tsp of ground cumin with the oregano, but it won't be the same as toasting the seeds really brings out their flavour. Place the cumin and oregano in a bowl and add all the other ingredients. Season and mix gently. If you want to make the salsa well ahead of time, mix everything except the avocado and wait until just before serving to add it, so that it does not get the chance to go brown.

Heat the oven to 200°C/400°F/gas 6/fan oven 180°C.

Place the chicken in a roasting tray. Mix the cumin and oregano in a cup. Rub the chicken skin first with the olive oil, then the cumin and oregano mixture, and finally sprinkle it with salt and pepper. Push the lime halves left over from the salsa into the cavity.

Roast the chicken for one hour, basting every 20 minutes. Remove from the oven, cover loosely with kitchen foil and leave it to rest for 15 minutes.

Carve the chicken and serve with any juices and the salsa.

CHICKEN AND AVOCADO SALAD
Ensalada de Pollo y Aguacate

A dish which encompasses three of the most Mexican of ingredients: chilli, sweetcorn and avocado, fire, sun and stone. It is sweet and spicy, chewy and smooth, colourful and bursting with flavour – perfect picnic food, whether packed into a container to carry in a rucksack, or in a nice bowl for a concert in the park – or of course sitting on a Caribbean beach and listening to the *mariachis* strumming their guitars and singing evocative Mexican songs! It is also very good mixed with pasta, or piled into a soft bread roll to make a *torta* (page 173). If you can't find a *poblano* chilli, use a green pepper and an extra chilli.

Serves 2

For the marinade:-
5 ml/1 tsp chipotle chilli sauce (see Resources)
5 ml/1 tsp olive oil
1 tsp cumin seeds, coarsely ground in a mortar or spice grinder
1 tsp fresh lime or lemon juice
½ tsp runny honey
1 red chilli, deseeded and finely sliced

2 large skinless, boneless chicken breasts
1 large poblano chilli (see Resources) or green pepper, about 200 g/7 oz
1 large red pepper, about 200 g/7 oz
1 tsp cumin seeds
40 g/1 ½ oz red onions, peeled and finely sliced
1 red and 1 green chilli, deseeded and finely sliced
5 ml/1 tsp chipotle chilli sauce (see Resources)
45 ml/3 tbsp olive oil
100 g/4 oz tinned or frozen sweetcorn, defrosted and well drained
1 tsp dried Mexican oregano (see Resources)
50 g/2 oz rocket or mixed salad leaves
Sea salt and freshly ground black pepper

1 x quantity Guacamole, without tomatoes or chillies (see page 159)

Whisk the ingredients for the marinade in a cup. Place the chicken in a small baking dish and pour the marinade over it. Set aside for at least a couple of hours

– the longer the better, and overnight in the refrigerator is ideal, but remember to bring it back to room temperature before cooking.

Heat the grill to high. Line the grill pan with foil and place the poblano chilli and red pepper on it. Grill them 10 cm/4 in from the heat, turning them as needed, until the skin is blistered and charred all over. Cool slightly, then peel, discard the stem, seeds and core, and cut into long strips about 1cm/½ in wide.

Toast the cumin seeds in a heavy frying pan over medium heat, stirring all the time, until they release their aroma – 2 to 3 minutes. Tip them into a mortar or spice grinder and grind them coarsely.

Heat the grill to high again and grill the chicken, still in its dish, 10 cm/4 in from the heat for about 5 minutes on each side, until firm and lightly caramelised. Cool completely and slice. Place in a roomy salad bowl and toss gently with the roasted poblano, red pepper and all the other ingredients except the rocket or salad leaves. Set aside until you are ready to eat – the flavours will mingle and mellow as it sits.

Mix in the rocket or salad leaves, top with the guacamole and serve immediately.

ROAST MEXICAN VEGETABLES WITH *GUACAMOLE* AND *TOMATILLO SALSA*

Verduras Asadas con Guacamole y Salsa Verde

One of the joys of this dish for me is that its ingredients are essentially native (except for the aubergine) and, other than the fact that nowadays they are fried, give one a clear idea of the type of food the Spanish found when they landed in the Americas. This is typical street stall food, with the vegetables gently browning and softening in a large frying pan on a back burner until they are crusty and their flavour is rich and concentrated. They are then served with warm tortillas – you can either roll them up into a *taco* or use the tortilla to scoop them up – and a variety of fresh, sharp salsas. The method works equally well of course with many other vegetables, such as winter roots – so if you are not in the mood for Mexican, try parsnips, Jerusalem artichokes, swedes and celeriac with the *guacamole* and *salsa*, it will be equally delicious.

Serves 2

400 g/14 oz aubergines, cut into 2 cm/¾ in pieces
375 g/13 oz poblano chillies (see Resources) or green peppers, cut into 1 cm/½ in wide strips
400 g/14 oz sweet potatoes, peeled and cut into 2 cm/¾ in pieces
250g/9 oz courgettes, cut into 1 cm/½ in rounds
400g/14 oz pumpkin, peeled, seeded and cut into 2 cm/¾ in pieces
60 ml/4 tbsp olive oil
2 large red chillies, deseeded and finely sliced
1 x quantity Guacamole (page 159)
1 x quantity Tomatillo Salsa (page 206)
Warm corn tortillas to serve
Sea salt and freshly ground black pepper

Heat the oven to 200°C/400°F/gas 6/fan oven 180°C. Place all the vegetables in a large roasting tin, season well, drizzle with olive oil and roast, stirring every 15 minutes or so, until they are soft, golden and crusty, about one hour.

Sprinkle with the sliced chillies and serve immediately with the guacamole, salsa and tortillas.

WILD MUSHROOM *TAMALES* WITH AVOCADO CREAM
Tamales de Hongos Silvestres y Chipotle con Crema de Aguacate

The autumn markets in the mountains are full of wild mushrooms, from the sinister corn fungus called *huitlacotchle* to the more familiar *chanterelles* and *pieds de mouton*, as well as many which I did not recognise, such as a bright yellow one in Pátzcuaro which the stall holder merely called *trompetita*, little trumpet. Having eaten these *tamales* in a fancy restaurant in Morelia, I tended to think of them as modern Mexican cooking, but on reflection realised that other than the crème fraîche in the sauce, it could easily be a pre-Hispanic dish, as wild mushrooms must have been plentiful in the woods and forests.

Makes 4 tamales

For the tamales:-
100 g/4 oz cornhusks (see Resources)
40 g/1 ½ oz butter, softened
1 tsp salt
½ tsp baking powder
1 tsp bouillon powder
125 g/4 ½ oz masa harina (see Resources)
200 ml/7 fl oz warm water
String (optional)

For the mushrooms:-
15 g/½ oz butter
100 g/4 oz onions, peeled and finely chopped
200 g/7 oz mixed wild mushrooms, cleaned
1 tsp chipotle chilli sauce (see Resources)
Sea salt and freshly ground black pepper

For the avocado cream:-
1 large ripe avocado
60 ml/¼ cup full fat crème fraîche
Sea salt and freshly ground black pepper

Put the cornhusks in a large bowl and pour a kettle of boiling water over them. Place a small saucepan lid on top of them to keep them submerged and leave them to soften and re-hydrate for a couple of hours or even overnight.

Melt the butter in a small frying pan, add the onions and cook gently until soft and translucent, about 10 minutes. Stir in the mushrooms, chilli sauce and some seasoning, and continue to cook until the mushrooms have released all their moisture and are starting to sizzle. Check the seasoning and set aside to cool.

For the tamales, place the butter, salt, baking and bouillon powders in a food processor and process until creamy and well blended. Add about a quarter of the masa harina followed by a quarter of the water, processing in between and repeating the procedure with the remaining masa harina and water until you have a thick batter.

Drain the cornhusks, lay them out on a dishcloth, cover them with a second dishcloth, and pat them dry. Arrange enough of them on the work surface to make a square about 15cm/6 in x 15cm/6 in, overlapping several pieces of husk if necessary. Spread a quarter of the batter on the square, leaving a 2 cm/¾ in border. Spoon a quarter of the mushrooms in the centre of the batter. Fold one side of the cornhusks up and over the batter and the filling, enclosing it all completely, then fold up the other side in the same way, to make a parcel. Don't worry if it is not particularly tidy, that is what tamales look like! Carefully pick the parcel up and set it aside, seam side down. Repeat with the rest of the batter and filling.

When the tamales are all made, they can either be steamed as they are, seam side down, or you can tie them up like a present, which makes them slightly easier to handle once they are cooked and improves the presentation. In Mexico, strips of cornhusk are used, which looks very ethnic and natural – but this also adds to the fiddliness of making tamales, so I use string.

Line a steamer with cornhusks or baking parchment and put it in a large saucepan with 3 cm/1 ¼ in of boiling water. Arrange the parcels in the steamer, cover the saucepan, and steam the tamales on low heat for 1 hour and 30 minutes.

Make the avocado cream shortly before serving. Halve the avocado, scoop the flesh into a food processor, add the crème fraîche and some salt and pepper, and process until very smooth. Check the seasoning.

Place one or two tamales on each plate and provide a pair of scissors to cut the string.

Add a dollop of avocado cream and serve immediately.

Any leftover cornhusks can be left to dry out completely and used on another occasion.

Huitlacoche

TROPICAL FRUIT AND AVOCADO SALAD
Ensalada de Fruta con Aguacate

A fruit salad with a difference! The acacia honey gives it an elusive perfume and the richness of the avocado balances the acidity of the fruit. The colours and textures are sensational. I was amazed when I ordered a fruit salad for breakfast and found that it had avocado in it, but of course avocado is a fruit, not a vegetable. Fruit salad does not benefit from sitting around anyway, but if you do decide to get ahead and make it several hours in advance, be sure not to add the avocado until the last moment so that it is bright green and does not soften too much. And obviously mix the salad very gently indeed to avoid mashing it.

Rolling the pomegranate around firmly on a work surface with the palm of your hand will loosen the seeds and make them much easier to remove. The pomegranate juice will stain your fingers but rubbing them with the squeezed lime halves will bring them back to normal.

Serves 6

2 pink grapefruit
90 ml/6 tbsp acacia honey
2 limes, juiced
1 pomegranate
1 small papaya
1 mango
½ small pineapple
1 large ripe avocado
15 g/½ oz mint, coarsely chopped plus a few small sprigs

Peel the grapefruit with a sharp knife, cut out the segments and place them in a roomy bowl. Squeeze the juice from the membrane into a cup, add the honey and lime juice, and whisk together into a syrup.

Halve the pomegranate, remove the seeds and add them to the grapefruit. Peel and deseed the papaya. Peel the mango and slice the flesh off the stone. Peel the pineapple and remove the core – remove the 'eyes' as well if you can be bothered Cut all three fruits into 2 cm/¾ in pieces and add to the grapefruit and pomegranate. The salad can be prepared up to this point several hours ahead.

Just before serving, stir the mint into the fruit. Peel and stone the avocado, dice the flesh into 1cm/½ in pieces, and sprinkle it over the other fruit in the bowl. Pour over the syrup and garnish with the mint sprigs.

Serve immediately.

AVOCADO AND ALMOND SMOOTHIE
Licuado de Aguacate y Almendras

Juice bars – *juguerías* – are found on virtually every street corner in Mexico, and offer such a huge variety and such unusual combinations that it is difficult to choose. Although they are all called juice – *jugo* – a lot of them are in fact smoothies, as the juice is not extracted from the fruit, rather the flesh is liquidised with some water or milk. It is well worth trying them on every available occasion, as they are prepared to order and beautifully fresh, with all their antioxidants and vitamins intact. I usually use soya milk and yoghurt for this recipe, making the smoothie vegan and free from saturated fat, without losing its wonderful richness. I love it for breakfast, as this pale green, lightly scented nectar is so sustaining that it sees me through to lunch time without hesitation.

Serves 1

1 large ripe avocado
250 ml/8 fl oz milk
100 ml/3 ½ fl oz plain yoghurt
30 ml/2 tbsp runny honey
Pinch of cinnamon powder
20 g/¾ oz toasted, flaked almonds + 1 tsp
A good squeeze of lime juice

Place all the ingredients except the teaspoon of almonds in a food processor or blender and blend until smooth. Pour into a glass and garnish with flaked almonds.

Drink immediately.

Diseño Maya

seed

Jitomates

From the seed sprang a vine with small golden fruit. It was a mere weed in the fields of corn and beans of the early Incas, barely valued as a food. But the seed slowly spread throughout the continent and when it reached Mexico, the Aztecs began to cultivate it and integrate it into their own cuisine. From there, it crossed an ocean aboard a Spanish galleon and, having landed in Spain, wove its magic throughout Europe and set off to conquer the rest of the world. Today, the Aztecs' *tomatl* is grown in virtually every country, from Iceland to the Falkland Islands, and is an intrinsic part of countless cuisines.

The tomato we are all most familiar with is red and round. Long tomatoes, and yellow tomatoes, started appearing in supermarkets a few years ago, but the tomato family is infinitely more exciting than we realise. West Dean Gardens in West Sussex grow countless varieties to exhibit at their annual Totally Tomato Show, and when I was researching a magazine article on tomatoes to coincide with the Show, I set off on a tomato discovery expedition. I was amazed to find that they come in all sorts of different shapes, sizes, colours, and even flavours – there are well over a hundred varieties of tomato and some of them are very exotic indeed. However, Mexicans cook with red tomatoes – big, juicy, sweet red tomatoes which positively sing with flavour. Their main role is in raw and cooked sauces: a bowl of *salsa cruda*, a fresh, tingling, aromatic mix of chopped tomatoes, onions, chilli and fresh coriander, appears as if by magic as soon as you sit down at a restaurant table, ready to be spooned onto *totopos*, tortilla chips, and munched while you decide what else to eat. The same *salsa* might appear as an accompaniment to grilled fish, stir-fried with some chicken strips, dolloped into soup or cooked with rice for *arroz a la mexicana* – a basic *salsa* of this sort is incredibly versatile. When it comes to cooked sauces, the tomatoes (as well as garlic cloves and chillies) are normally dry-roasted in a hot frying pan – this deepens and concentrates their flavour and gives them a delicious hint of wood smoke and burnt sugar; however, after much experimenting, I have come to the conclusion that grilling them and particularly roasting them in the oven is easier and works just as well, if not better.

Another type of 'tomato' is also extensively used in Mexican cooking: the *tomatillo* or 'green husked tomato' – which is not actually a tomato at all but a member of the physalis or Chinese gooseberry family. I have in fact used Chinese gooseberries on a few occasions when I have not been able to source *tomatillos*, with very acceptable results. *Tomatillos* have a lovely bite to them, sharp and tangy, reminiscent of citrus and green apples. They are used in exactly the same way as tomatoes and, yet again, essentially in sauces. Sadly, they are not always easy to find – I have come across them in large supermarkets and specialist food shops, but their presence on the high street is very restricted indeed. However, I have often found them at farmers' markets and farm shops, and they are available by mail order throughout the year and particularly during the growing season from July to October. Friends have grown them successfully in their gardens and green houses, and my own first attempt last summer in my diminutive garden produced enough *tomatillos* for three or four batches of sauce, which was a tremendous thrill; and I have no doubt that next year will be even better.

Tomatillos, just like Chinese gooseberries, are encased in a thin, papery husk which needs to be peeled away. A ripe *tomatillo* will fill its envelope quite snugly, almost to the point of bursting out of it, so reject any which are too small for their husks as they will have a lot of acidity and little flavour. The surface of a *tomatillo* is faintly sticky, so always rinse it before use.

Tomatillos are well worth tracking down or growing if you want a genuine taste of Mexico – and they freeze well. See Resources for *tomatillo* seeds.

If a recipe with a *tomatillo* sauce appeals but you have no *tomatillos* to hand, don't hesitate to try it with one of the tomato sauces – it will obviously not be the same but will still be totally delicious.

RAW TOMATO *SALSA*
Salsa Cruda

Fresh and gloriously aromatic, this is the most common of Mexican *salsas*. If you want to be traditional, you will need to pound it in a mortar, a *molcajete,* and the fragrance which rises from the ingredients as you crush them all together will make the whole exercise into a heady and utterly sensuous experience. The next best thing is to chop it all up on a chopping board – and your knife will need to be really sharp or it will just mash the tomatoes. I give in gracefully to the 21st century and simply make it in my food processor.

25 g/1 oz red onions, peeled and coarsely chopped
1 garlic clove, peeled
1 red and 1 green chilli, halved and deseeded
30 ml/2 tbsp olive oil
15g/½ oz fresh coriander
250 g/9 oz ripe tomatoes, quartered
Sea salt and freshly ground black pepper

Place the onions, garlic, chillies, coriander and olive oil in a food processor and process until coarsely chopped. Add some seasoning and the tomatoes, and process again for just a few seconds, to break down the tomatoes – you are looking for a chunky texture, not a purée. Scrape into a bowl and check the seasoning.

The salsa can be prepared a couple of hours ahead of time, but after that it becomes a bit watery. If you are not going to eat it immediately, don't add any salt until you are ready to serve.

COOKED TOMATO SAUCES

Rather than searing tomatoes, chillies and garlic on a hot, dry griddle like a Mexican cook, I grill or roast them: it is easier and less hassle, and it produces a better sauce, as northern tomatoes do not have quite the flavour of Mexican ones and grilling or roasting them concentrates whatever flavour they have – roasting will turn even the dullest tomato into a bold, strong sauce. You will need fewer tomatoes for a grilled tomato sauce, as they do not dehydrate quite as much under a grill as during a prolonged session in the oven, but on the other hand, dehydration not only strengthens the flavour but also produces a wonderfully velvety texture. It boils down in the end to a question of time, so I roast if I can, grill when I cannot. And as with the raw sauce, I use a food processor.

I often promise myself to make my tomato sauces traditionally, grinding them by hand rather than puréeing them mechanically. Los Colorines Restaurant in Tepoztlán nestles under the great rocky crags high above the valley of Cuernavaca, and serves outstanding, authentic, uncompromising Mexican food; I say uncompromising because the village attracts a lot of tourists, many of them New Age, but the restaurant menu is as un-touristy as you can get. I wandered through a back courtyard and came across a cook preparing tomatoes for a sauce. She was kneeling in front of a huge slab of lava rock, a *metate*, and grinding a mountain of tomatoes down with a stone rolling pin, pushing them over the edge of the *metate* into a plastic bucket when she had achieved the right texture. As I quietly watched her, I realised that tomato sauces had been made in this way for hundreds if not thousands of years. I commented to her that this was a labour intensive way of working, but she just smiled and replied *"en México, así se hace"*, this is how it is done in Mexico.

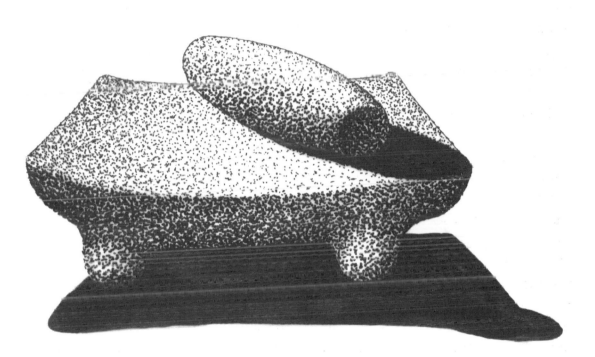

Metate.

GRILLED TOMATO SAUCE

500 g/18 oz tomatoes, halved
8 garlic cloves, unpeeled
45 ml/3 tbsp olive oil
250 g/9 oz onions, peeled and coarsely chopped
Sea salt and freshly ground black pepper

Heat the grill to high. Line the grill pan with foil and arrange the tomatoes, cut side up, and garlic cloves on it. Grill 10 cm/4 in from the heat for about 20 minutes, until lightly charred, turning the garlic cloves over half way through. Cool, then peel the garlic cloves and place them in a food processor with the tomatoes and any juices. Process to a chunky purée.

While the tomatoes are grilling, heat the olive oil in a frying pan and cook the onions until soft and golden. Add the tomato purée and some seasoning, and cook over medium heat for about 15 minutes, stirring often, until nice and thick.

ROAST TOMATO SAUCE

This is my preferred way of making a Mexican tomato sauce. It requires less attention than the grilling method, but it does take longer. However, the addition of honey in this recipe enhances the tomato flavour very considerably – and you can't add honey in the grilled recipe as it tends to burn before the tomatoes have softened. You also need more tomatoes to make the same amount of sauce, as they lose most of their moisture.

1 kg/2 ¼ lb tomatoes, halved
6 large garlic cloves, peeled and finely sliced
10 ml/2 tsp runny honey
45 ml/3 tbsp olive oil
250 g/9 oz onions, peeled and coarsely chopped
Sea salt and freshly ground black pepper

Heat the oven to 200°C/400°F/gas 6/fan oven 180°C.

Put the tomatoes cut side up in a roasting tray lined with foil and push the garlic slivers into the seedy bits. Drizzle first with honey and then 2 tbsp of olive oil. Season well and cook for one hour, until soft and slightly blackened. Cool for 10 minutes then place in a food processor and process to a chunky purée.

While the tomatoes are roasting, heat the remaining 15 ml/1 tbsp of olive oil in a frying pan and cook the onions until soft and golden. Add the tomato purée and some seasoning, and cook over medium heat for about 15 minutes, stirring often, until nice and thick.

ROASTED TOMATOES

The recipe for the roast tomato sauce above does not work with all chillies, because each chilli has its own unique degree of sweetness and fire and different levels of flavour. These roast tomatoes are therefore a building base for chilli and tomato sauces – apart from the fact that they are delicious on their own, on toast, in pasta or in a salad.

1 kg/2 ¼ lb tomatoes, halved
6 large garlic cloves, peeled and finely sliced
10 ml/2 tsp runny honey
30 ml/2 tbsp olive oil
Sea salt and freshly ground black pepper

Heat the oven to 200°C/400°F/gas 6/fan oven 180°C.

Put the tomatoes cut side up in a roasting tray lined with foil and push the garlic slivers into the seedy bits. Drizzle first with honey and then olive oil. Season well and cook for one hour, until soft and slightly blackened.

TOMATILLO SAUCES

Two sharp, green, brightly flavoured sauces. The cooked one is even better when combined with cream and cheese – the richness is tempered and lightened by the *tomatillo's* natural acidity, resulting in a sauce which is soft, mellow and sparkling at the same time. If you cannot find *tomatillos* at your local farmers' market or supermarket, see Resources for mail order alternatives.

TOMATILLO SALSA
Salsa Verde Cruda

300 g/11 oz tomatillos, husked and rinsed
50 g/2 oz onions, peeled and coarsely chopped
1 large mild red chilli, deseeded and chopped
15 g/½ oz fresh coriander
Sea salt and freshly ground black pepper

Chop the tomatillos coarsely. Put them in a food processor with all the other ingredients and whizz up for a few seconds, until broken down but still a bit chunky. The salsa can be made several hours in advance.

COOKED TOMATILLO SAUCE
Salsa Verde Cocida

500 g/18 oz tomatillos, husked and rinsed
3 mild green chillies
3 garlic cloves, unpeeled
30 ml/2 tbsp olive oil
100 g/4 oz onions, peeled and coarsely chopped
Sea salt and freshly ground black pepper

Heat the grill to high. Line the grill pan with foil and arrange the tomatillos, chillies and garlic on it. Grill 10 cm / 4 in from the heat for about 10 minutes, until lightly browned, then turn them all over and grill the other side in the same way. Set aside to cool, then peel the garlic, and halve and deseed the chillies. Place them in a food processor with the tomatillos and any juices and process to a chunky purée.

While the vegetables are grilling, heat the olive oil in a frying pan and fry the onions until soft and starting to brown. Add the tomatillo purée and some seasoning, and cook over low heat for about 15 minutes, stirring often, until nice and thick.

COOKED *CHIPOTLE* SAUCE
Salsa de Chipotle Cocida

This is the most useful tomato sauce because, although it is flavoured with *chipotle*, it does not involve toasting and rehydrating the dried chilli – the wonderful smoky flavour and heat come from a jar, and if you are pushed for time, you can still create a traditional Mexican sauce without feeling that you are cheating.

500 g/18 oz tomatoes, halved
8 garlic cloves, unpeeled
45 ml/3 tbsp olive oil
250 g/9 oz onions, peeled and coarsely chopped
15 ml/1 tbsp chipotle chilli sauce (see Resources)
Sea salt and freshly ground black pepper

Heat the grill to high. Line the grill pan with foil and place the tomato halves, cut side up, and garlic cloves on it. Grill 10 cm/4 in from the heat for about 20 minutes, until soft and slightly blackened, turning the garlic cloves over half way through. Cool, then peel the garlic and place it in a food processor with the tomatoes and any juices. Process to a chunky purée.

While the tomatoes are grilling, heat the olive oil in a frying pan and cook the onions until soft and golden. Add the tomato purée, the chipotle chilli sauce and some seasoning, and cook over medium heat for about 15 minutes, stirring often, until nice and thick.

NOODLE AND TOMATO SOUP

Sopa de Fideos

I had this soup for supper at least three times a week throughout my childhood – an incredibly soothing, nourishing dish, perfect in its simplicity. It is a distinct hybrid from both Old and New Worlds, as *fideos* are very thin pasta, rather like the Italian angel hair or vermicelli. You can use spaghetti but in that case cook it for at least double the normal time. Heavier pastas such as penne are not suitable, they are just too Italian.

Serves 2

30 ml/2 tbsp olive oil
200 g/7 oz onions, peeled and coarsely chopped
½ x quantity Roasted Tomatoes (page 205)
1 litre/1 ¾ pints water
100 g/4 oz angel hair pasta or vermicelli
1 tbsp chopped parsley
Sea salt and freshly ground black pepper

Heat the oil in a large, heavy-bottomed saucepan and cook the onions, stirring every now and then, until soft and golden, about 20 minutes. Scrape into a food processor, add the tomatoes, and process to a chunky purée. Return the mixture to the frying pan and stir-fry for 5 minutes, until it thickens slightly. Add the water and bring to the boil. Break the pasta up with your hands into pieces about 5 cm/2 in long and add to the tomato broth. Simmer, covered, for 6 minutes – the pasta needs to be really soft.

Check the seasoning, stir in the parsley and serve immediately.

MEXICAN SALAD
Ensalada Mexicana

A rather vague name, which could mean anything – it appears on restaurant menus without any accompanying explanation, and what you see when it is put in front of you is what you get. Although the ingredients can vary, it always seems to feature tomatoes, onions, chillies, and cheese, whether fresh, sharp and crumbly, or well aged, mellow and savoury. One of the most popular components is French beans; another is cactus paddles, which are sold in great piles in the markets, and the sight of little girls sitting by their mothers, learning at an early age to slice off the thorns, is very common and very Mexican. Once disarmed, the paddles are sliced and boiled; their texture is very reminiscent of French beans, their flavour faintly more lemony.

This salad does not sit well, as the tomatoes tend to go watery, so assemble it just before you are ready to eat.

Serves 4

250 g/9 oz French beans, topped, tailed and cut in half
225 g/8 oz red cherry tomatoes, quartered
50 g/2 oz red onions, peeled and finely sliced
2 garlic cloves, peeled and crushed
1 hot red and 1 hot green chilli, deseeded and finely sliced
3 tbsp/45 ml olive oil
75 g/3 oz Parmesan cheese, freshly grated
20 g/¾ oz fresh coriander or flat leaf parsley, coarsely chopped
Sea salt and freshly ground black pepper

Cook the beans in plenty of salted, boiling water until just tender, about 5 minutes depending on their thickness. Drain, refresh in cold water, and drain again, shaking out any excess moisture. Place them in a clean dishcloth and set aside while you assemble the rest of the salad.

In a roomy bowl, mix the tomatoes, onions, garlic, chillies, olive oil and some seasoning. Stir in the beans. Sprinkle with the cheese and herbs and toss gently.

Serve immediately.

PRAWN COCKTAIL
Coctel de Camarones

Mexico has thousands of kilometres of coastline and a fabulous fish cuisine to go with it. Seafood cocktails feature on every seaside menu, from oysters with little more than a squeeze of lime juice and a sprinkling of fresh coriander, to sophisticated medleys of molluscs, crustaceans and some kind of smoked fish. They are colourful, brightly flavoured and wonderfully fresh. I remember eating this prawn cocktail countless times during school holidays at the beach; it was sometimes garnished with a dollop of pink mayonnaise which I fastidiously scraped off to ensure that its cloying, ketchupy sweetness did not mask the pristine taste of land and sea.

You can use cooked prawns but they just don't seem to soak up the flavours in the same way.

Serves 2

1 tsp cumin seeds
90 ml/6 tbsp olive oil
200 g/7 oz raw king prawns, shelled and deveined
50 g/2 oz red onions, peeled and finely chopped
1 garlic clove, peeled and crushed
125 g/4 ½ oz cherry tomatoes, quartered – a mixture of red and yellow looks very pretty
1 large ripe avocado, peeled and cut into 1 cm/½ in pieces
2 limes
15 g/½ oz fresh coriander, coarsely chopped
2 large Cos lettuce leaves, finely sliced
Sea salt and freshly ground black pepper

Toast the cumin seeds in a heavy frying pan over medium heat, stirring all the time, until they release their aroma – 2 to 3 minutes. Tip them into a mortar and grind coarsely with a pestle; you can do this in a spice grinder but make sure you keep some texture.

Heat the olive oil in a frying pan, add the cumin and cook for one minute. Add the prawns and stir-fry over medium heat until they just turn pink. Season and cool for 10 minutes.

Mix the onions, garlic, tomatoes, avocado and the juice of one lime in a bowl. Carefully fold in the prawns and their juices. Cut the second lime in half. Make a bed of shredded lettuce on two plates, pile the prawn cocktail on top and sprinkle with coriander.

Garnish with lime halves and serve immediately.

QUESADILLA AND TOMATO SALAD
Ensalada de Tomate y Quesadilla

This is *quesadillas* at their simplest, an *antojito*, a snack, eaten at every street stall – there is little preparation involved and they can be put together, cooked and served with a spoonful of basic *salsa* in minutes (by an experienced Mexican street cook anyway!). I rather like them with a chunky tomato salad instead of a *salsa*. The filling will invariably contain cheese (*queso* is Spanish for cheese), which will melt as the *quesadilla* is cooked, providing a lovely contrast to the crisp tortilla envelope.

Makes 4 quesadillas and serves 2 as a light lunch or 4 as a first course

For the tomato salad:-
300 g/11 oz tomatoes, thickly sliced
40 g/1 ½ oz red onions, peeled and finely chopped
1 garlic clove, peeled and crushed
1 red chilli, deseeded and finely sliced
15 g/½ oz mint, coarsely chopped
60 ml/4 tbsp olive oil
1 lime, quartered
2 good handfuls rocket
Sea salt and freshly ground black pepper

For the quesadillas:-
100 g/4 oz fresh goat's cheese
50 g/2 oz Farmhouse Cheddar cheese, coarsely grated
20 g/¾ oz red onions, peeled and finely chopped
2 corn tortillas

For the dressing:-
45 ml/3 tbsp olive oil
½ lime, juiced
5 ml/1 tsp chipotle chilli sauce (see Resources)

Gently mix all the ingredients for the salad except the lime wedges, rocket and seasoning in a bowl and set aside while you make the quesadillas.

Mash the goat's cheese in a small bowl and fold in the Cheddar cheese and onions. Lay the two tortillas out on a work surface. Spread half the cheese mixture over one half of each tortilla. Fold each tortilla in half, into a half-moon shape, and press it down gently with a spatula.

Heat a large, heavy frying pan over medium heat and place the quesadillas in it, curved edges facing outwards. Cook for about 4 minutes, until lightly browned, then carefully flip them over and brown the other side.

While the quesadillas are cooking, whisk the olive oil, lime juice and chipotle chilli sauce in a cup or small bowl to make the dressing. Season the tomato salad. Divide the rocket between two or four plates and top with the salad.

When the quesadillas are hot and crusty, lift them with a spatula onto a chopping board and cut them in half with a sharp knife, into fan shapes. Place them on top of the tomato salad and drizzle with the chipotle dressing.

Garnish with lime wedges and serve immediately.

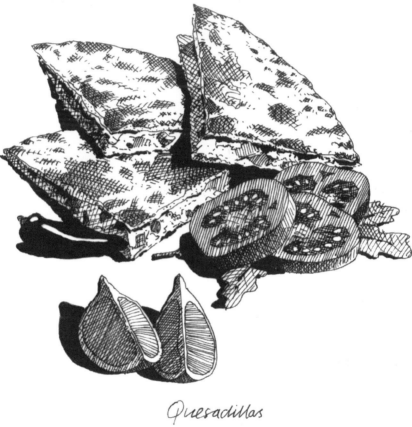

Quesadillas

ROAST TOMATOES WITH MULTI-COLOURED *RAJAS* AND MANGO *SALSA*

Tomates Asados con Rajas y Mango

This salad makes a lovely first course or light lunch. The combination of the sharp tomatoes, bitter peppers, spicy chillies and sweet salsa is fantastic and the colours even more so. The dish struck me as being somewhat *nouvelle cuisine* when I came across it on the menu of a rather fancy restaurant on the Pacific coast, but having tasted it, I was totally won over as the flavours are truly Mexican, if decidedly modern.

Serves 2 as a light lunch

250 g/9 oz red cherry tomatoes, halved
5 ml/1 tsp honey
75 ml/5 tbsp olive oil
1 x quantity Multi-coloured Rajas (page 103)
15 g/½ oz fresh coriander, coarsely chopped
2 good handfuls rocket
Sea salt and freshly ground black pepper
Warm corn tortillas or crusty bread, to serve

For the mango salsa:-
1 large mango, peeled and diced
75 g/3 oz red onions, peeled and finely chopped
1 garlic clove, peeled and crushed
1 red chilli, deseeded and finely sliced
45 ml/3 tbsp olive oil
15 ml/1 tbsp fresh lime juice, about ½ lime
Salt and freshly ground black pepper

Heat the oven to 200°C/400°F/gas 6/fan oven 180°C.

Arrange the tomato halves, cut side up and close together, in a roasting tray lined with foil and drizzle first with honey, then 1 tbsp of olive oil. Season well and bake for 30 to 45 minutes, until soft and lightly caramelised. Cool and place in a large bowl.

For the mango salsa, mix all the ingredients in a small bowl. The salsa will sit happily for an hour or two.

Carefully stir the remaining olive oil, the rajas, the coriander and some seasoning into the tomatoes.

Place the rocket on two plates, top with the tomato and rajas salad and serve immediately with the mango salsa and warm tortillas or bread to soak up the delicious juices.

FRIED EGGS WITH BRICKLAYER'S SAUCE
Huevos del Albañil

I have not so far managed to find out why this dish is attributed to bricklayers, but whoever the bricklayers were, they could certainly cook! The play of textures and flavours between the sharpness of the sauce, the mellowness of the cream, the saltiness of the cheese and the richness of the avocado really keeps the palate on its toes and shows off the versatility of *tomatillos* to perfection. This is a typical, traditional breakfast throughout the country, although a popular variation is to toss some stale tortillas into the sauce to make green *chilaquiles* which serve as a bed for the eggs.

Serves 2

1 x quantity Tomatillo Salsa (page 206), heated
1 small ripe avocado, peeled and cut into 1 cm/½ in dice
15 g/½ oz fresh coriander, coarsely chopped
100 ml/3 ½ fl oz vegetable oil
4 eggs
100 ml/3 ½ fl oz single cream
30 g/1 ¼ oz Feta cheese
Sea salt and freshly ground black pepper

Have the salsa, avocado and coriander ready.

Heat the oil in a non-stick frying pan and fry the eggs sunny side up.
Place them on warm plates, season them lightly, drizzle with the cream, crumble over the Feta cheese, and sprinkle with coriander and avocado.

Serve immediately with the salsa on the side.

BREAD ROLLS WITH MEXICAN EGGS
Tortas de Huevos a la Mexicana

Three specific bread rolls are used in Mexico: oval *bolillos* and round *regueletes* are served as an accompaniment to food, rather like French bread; *teleras* are larger and flatter, with two slashes across the top, and perfect for filling. All three have a lovely crisp crust and a fairly dense crumb. I usually use rolls called *grand rustique* as the texture is vaguely similar, and they are big enough to accommodate the huge amount of filling which Mexican cooks manage to stuff into their *tortas*. You can also use a *ciabatta* loaf and slice it into individual portions once filled, or *petits pains* – *ciabatta* rolls are not really suitable as they have very little crumb. *Huevos a la Mexicana* are a simple scrambled egg dish, lightly spiced and very popular for breakfast.

Makes 2 large rolls

30 ml/2 tbsp olive oil
50 g/2 oz onions, peeled and coarsely chopped
1 red chilli, deseeded and finely sliced
75 g/3 oz tomatoes, coarsely chopped
4 eggs
2 large crisp bread rolls, halved
Sea salt and freshly ground black pepper

Heat the oil in a medium saucepan, add the onions and chilli, and cook over moderate heat for about 10 minutes, until soft and starting to brown. Add the tomatoes and some seasoning, and cook for a further 10 minutes to evaporate any excess moisture.

Break the eggs into the tomato mixture and stir them around vigorously to break them up and scramble them. Continue cooking over gentle heat until they form soft, moist curds.

Check the seasoning and pile into the bread rolls.

Eat immediately.

If you are intending to take the tortas on a picnic – and they are lovely picnic food because the flavours all seep into the bread – let the eggs cool before making the tortas.

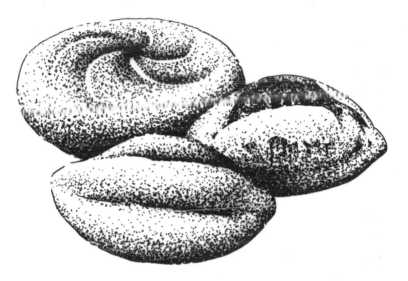

Pán Mexicano

STUFFED MUSHROOMS
Hongos Rellenos

The summer rains in Mexico slashed across the street every afternoon at the same time. The downpours were so heavy that we could not hold up an umbrella, but they were so predictable that we were prepared and made sure we were not caught out in the open. Global warming seems to be extending the rainy season and even October can now be very wet in the afternoon and early evening. One of the main beneficiaries of this increasing moisture is the mushroom season, with the damp forested mountains offering their crop of wild fungi for almost half the year.

If you have any Mexican Rice left over from another meal, these delectable mushrooms are quick and easy to make. It is a dish full of contrasts: the sharp tomato sauce, the hint of smoky *chipotle*, the sweet plantain, the rich, savoury chorizo, the tangy cheese. I love to serve them with the sweet potato purée on page 153.

Serves 2/4

100 g/4 oz chorizo sausage, diced
1 large ripe plantain, about 250 g/9 oz
60 ml/4 tbsp vegetable oil
½ x quantity Mexican Rice (page 232)
1 heaped tsp chipotle chilli sauce (see Resources)
100 g/4 oz Feta cheese
4 large portabello mushrooms, peeled
30 ml/2 tbsp olive oil
75 g/3 oz Farmhouse Cheddar cheese, coarsely grated
Sea salt and freshly ground black pepper

Heat a small, non-stick frying pan and cook the chorizo over medium heat, stirring occasionally, until it has released most of its fat and is golden, about 10 minutes. With a slotted spoon, remove it to a plate lined with kitchen paper to drain. Discard the fat and wipe out the frying pan.

While the chorizo is cooking, peel the plantain and dice it. The easiest way to do this is to quarter it lengthways and then slice it across about ¾ cm/1/3 in thick. Heat the vegetable oil in the frying pan and cook the plantain over highish heat until golden – keep stirring as it tends to stick. With a slotted spoon, scoop it out onto another plate lined with kitchen paper to drain.

Put the rice in a large bowl and gently mix in the chorizo, plantain, chipotle chilli sauce and Feta cheese.

Heat the oven to 200°C/400°F/gas 6/fan oven 180°C.

Arrange the mushrooms, stalk side up, in a gratin dish, season them and drizzle with the olive oil. Top them with the rice mixture (a large pastry ring is invaluable here but don't try to make them look tidy, that is very unMexican!) and sprinkle them with the Cheddar cheese.

Bake for 30 minutes and serve immediately, although they are actually terribly good cold as well.

PUMPKIN STEW
Guisado de Calabaza

Pumpkins and squashes can be rather insipid, to say the least, and roasting them really concentrates their flavour and firms their texture. It also, however, emphasizes their sweetness which can sometimes be rather cloying, hence my addition of limes at the roasting stage; this not only takes the edge off any sweetness but also adds an extra dimension of flavour, as the roasted limes are utterly delicious – so don't under any circumstances discard them. The version of pumpkin stew which we ate in Puebla, the great gastronomic centre of Mexico, was fried and then tossed in plenty of lime juice, which was very tasty, but I think that somehow my idea of roasting limes with the vegetables has made it that much better! The chillies in the topping need to be quite hot, yet again to cut through the sweetness of the pumpkin. If you cannot find a *poblano* chilli, a green pepper will do.

Serves 4

1.5 kg pumpkin or butternut squash, peeled, deseeded and cut into 2.5 cm/1 in pieces
2 limes, quartered
60 ml/4 tbsp olive oil
1 large poblano chilli (see Resources) or green pepper, about 200 g/7 oz, cut into 1 cm/½ in wide strips
1 large red pepper, about 200 g/7 oz, cut into 1 cm/½ in wide strips
350 g/12 oz onions, peeled and coarsely chopped
500 g/18 oz tomatoes, coarsely chopped
15 ml/1 tbsp chipotle chilli sauce (see Resources)
15 g/½ oz fresh coriander leaves
Sea salt and freshly ground black pepper

For the Feta salsa:-
1 large red and 1 large green chilli, medium hot, deseeded and finely sliced
75 g/3 oz red onions, peeled and finely chopped
1 large garlic clove, peeled and crushed

15 ml/1 tbsp fresh lime juice
30 ml/2 tbsp olive oil
15 g/½ oz fresh coriander, coarsely chopped
100 g/4 oz Feta cheese, crumbled

Heat the oven to 200°C/400°F/Gas 6/fan oven 180°C.

Place the pumpkin and lime quarters in an ovenproof dish, drizzle with 30 ml/2 tbsp of olive oil, season well, and roast in the oven until the pumpkin is soft and starting to blacken at the edges – this will take about one hour, depending on how watery the pumpkin was to start with. Give it all a stir every now and then. Do the same with the poblano chilli and red pepper: place them in another ovenproof dish, drizzle with 15 ml/1 tbsp of olive oil, season them, and roast, stirring occasionally, until starting to blacken along the edges, about 30 minutes.

Heat the remaining olive oil in a frying pan and fry the onions gently, stirring regularly, until soft and golden, about 15 minutes. Add the tomatoes, the chipotle chilli sauce and some seasoning, and cook until the tomatoes have broken down and most of the moisture has evaporated. Stir in the pumpkin, limes, poblano chilli and red pepper. Check the seasoning and add a bit more chipotle chilli sauce if it is not spicy enough for you.

The stew can be prepared up to this point ahead of time, cooled and refrigerated. Reheat gently before serving.

For the salsa, mix all the ingredients together gently in a small bowl.

Stir the coriander leaves into the stew and divide it between four warm plates. Spoon the Feta salsa over the top.

Serve immediately.

MUSSELS IN CREAMY *SALSA VERDE*
Mejillones en Salsa Verde con Crema

The cooking juices from the mussels blend with the cream and *tomatillos*, coating the mussels in a rich, luscious, tangy sauce which beats the Norman *moules à la crème* hands down, although crisp rolls or French bread are much better than tortillas for soaking up the sauce! Mussels can be a pain to prepare, as you need a lot of them, even for just two people, and scraping the barnacles off them and de-bearding them is time-consuming and frustrating. However, you will not regret the effort and many fishmongers and supermarkets now sell them scraped and ready to cook. Be sure to discard any that float, feel very light (empty!), extra heavy (full of sand!), or do not close when tapped sharply with the handle of a spoon (very dead!).

Serves 2

500 g/18 oz tomatillos, husked and rinsed
2 hot green chillies
4 garlic cloves, unpeeled
30 ml/2 tbsp olive oil
175 g/6 oz onions, peeled and coarsely chopped
250 ml/8 fl oz extra thick double cream
1 kg/2 ¼ lb shell-on mussels, scrubbed and de-bearded
15 g/½ oz fresh coriander, coarsely chopped
Crisp rolls or French bread, to serve

Heat the grill to high. Line the grill pan with foil and arrange the tomatillos, chillies and garlic on it. Grill 10 cm/4 in from the heat for about 10 minutes, until lightly browned, then turn them all over and grill the other side in the same way. Set aside to cool, then peel the garlic and halve and deseed the chillies. Place them in a food processor with the tomatillos and any juices and process to a chunky purée.

While the vegetables are grilling, heat the olive oil in a big saucepan and fry the onions until soft and starting to brown, about 15 minutes. Add the tomatillo purée and some seasoning, and cook over low heat for about 20 minutes, stirring occasionally, until thick. Stir in the cream.

While the sauce is cooking, check the mussels and discard any open ones. Place them on top of the sauce in the saucepan, cover the pan and cook over high heat for about 3 minutes, shaking the pan occasionally, until they open. With a large spoon, turn them over and over in the sauce to coat them well.

Serve immediately in deep bowls, sprinkled with coriander, with rolls or bread to soak up the sauce.

Cazuela, mejillones y tomatillos

MACKEREL VERACRUZ-STYLE
Pescado a la Veracruzana

In the bustling, raffish port of Veracruz, a whole red snapper, *huachinango*, is used, and very beautiful it looks too, sitting on a large serving plate surrounded by its red, slightly herby, distinctly tangy sauce. Mackerel is an excellent fish to use in this dish, because its oily, rich flesh balances the bite of the olives, capers and vinegary chillies. Unusually for a Mexican tomato sauce, this one does not griddle the tomatoes but cooks them Italian-style in a frying pan. Bottled *jalapeño* chillies are available in the "world foods" section of most supermarkets.

Large sardines can be used instead of mackerel, although I find that their many bones make them frustrating to eat. Sea bass is also good, but its delicate flesh can be overpowered by the gutsy sauce.

Serves 2

30 ml/2 tbsp olive oil
125 g/4 ½ oz onions, peeled and chopped
2 garlic cloves, peeled and crushed
500 g/18 oz tomatoes, skinned and coarsely chopped
1 bay leaf
1 heaped tsp dried Mexican oregano (see Resources)
5 ml/1 tsp runny honey
½ tsp ground cinnamon
10 green olives, pitted and halved
1 heaped tbsp capers, rinsed and squeezed dry
1 pickled jalapeño chilli, rinsed and finely sliced
2 large mackerel, cleaned
15 g/½ oz flat leaf parsley, coarsely chopped
Sea salt and freshly ground black pepper

Heat the oil in a frying pan and cook the onions and garlic until soft and golden, about 15 minutes. Add the tomatoes, bay leaf, oregano, honey, cinnamon and some seasoning, and simmer, uncovered, for about 20 minutes, until the moisture from the tomatoes has evaporated and the sauce is nice and thick. Add the olives, capers and chilli and cook for a further 5 minutes.

Heat the oven to 200°C/400°F/gas 6/fan oven180°C. Make 3 diagonal slashes on one side of the mackerel and place them, slashed side up, in a baking dish. Pour the sauce over them and bake them for 15 minutes.

Sprinkle with parsley and serve immediately.

BRAISED CHICKEN IN *CHORIZO* SAUCE
Estofado de Pollo con Chorizo

This tomato sauce is flavoured with chorizo and roast garlic, and then blended to a purée, making it rich, spicy and deeply savoury. The origins of the dish are obviously Spanish, as chicken. pigs and garlic all landed on Mexican beaches with the *Conquistadores*, but the roasting of the garlic and tomatoes is quintessentially Mexican, and the smoky smoothness of the chilli establishes it firmly in *la cocina mexicana*.

10 garlic cloves, unpeeled
100 g/4 oz chorizo sausage, diced
1 chicken, jointed into 8 pieces
30 ml/2 tbsp olive oil
225 g/8 oz onions, peeled and coarsely chopped
450 g/1 lb tomatoes, skinned and coarsely chopped
15 ml/1 tbsp chipotle chilli sauce (see Resources)
500 ml/17 fl oz chicken or vegetable stock or water with 1 tsp bouillon powder
Sea salt and freshly ground black pepper

Heat the oven to 200°C/400°F/gas 6/fan oven 180°C.

Place the garlic cloves on a baking tray and cook them in the oven for 30 minutes. Check them to make sure they are nice and soft – if they are still a bit hard, return them to the oven for a further 10 minutes. Set them aside to cool.

Cook the chorizo in a dry heavy frying pan until it has released most of its fat and is golden, about 10 minutes. With a slotted spoon, remove it to a large plate lined with kitchen paper to drain.

Brown the chicken pieces all over in the chorizo fat, then remove them to a plate.

Discard the fat, wipe out the frying pan and heat 2 tbsp of olive oil in it. Add the onions and cook over medium heat until translucent and just starting to brown. Squeeze the garlic cloves from their skins and add them to the onions. Raise the heat to high, stir in the tomatoes, chorizo and chipotle chilli sauce, and cook for 5 minutes, to break the tomatoes down. Pour in the stock and cook the sauce fairly briskly until it is well reduced and thick, about 10 minutes. Cool slightly, then purée in a food processor or blender.

Return the sauce to the pan, add some seasoning and the chicken pieces, cover the pan, reduce the heat to low and cook for 30 minutes. Check the seasoning and add a bit more chilli sauce if it is not spicy enough for you.

Serve immediately or cool and refrigerate. The flavour improves with keeping.

DUCK WITH *TROPICANA SALSA* AND MEXICAN RICE
Pato con Arroz a la Mexicana y Salsa Tropicana

Rice is a Spanish contribution to Mexican cuisine and, rather like tortillas, is served with virtually everything, either plain or flavoured with tomatoes, bean broth, puréed chillies, strips of *poblano* chilli, fried plantains, spices... I like my *arroz a la mexicana* with a strong tomato flavour, so I use a lot of cooked tomato sauce in the base, which gives the final dish a moist texture, reminiscent of Italian risotto – and I go for very un-Mexican brown rice. We came across the *salsa* at a beachside restaurant in Uxmal, on the Caribbean coast – we sat under a palm-frond umbrella, looking out over the turquoise sea, our feet buried in pure white sand, and ate plain grilled prawns with *salsa tropicana* – utterly wonderful. The restaurant's version included grated fresh coconut but, as ever, I looked for a simpler substitute and found that coconut cream is a perfect alternative.

Serves 2

For the rice:-
30 ml/2 tbsp olive oil
250 g/8 oz brown basmati rice
1 x quantity Grilled Tomato Sauce (page 204)
1 tbsp bouillon powder
400 ml/14 fl oz boiling water
Sea salt and freshly ground black pepper

For the tropicana salsa:-
50 g/2 oz coconut cream, chopped or coarsely grated
2 garlic cloves, peeled
2 hot green chillies, halved and deseeded
1 fat spring onion, coarsely chopped
200 ml/7 fl oz olive oil
1 lime, juiced
30 g/1 ¼ oz fresh coriander
100 g/4 oz roasted, salted peanuts

1 medium mango, peeled and diced
Sea salt and freshly ground black pepper

For the duck:-
15 ml/1 tbsp olive oil
2 duck breast fillets, with skin, about 200 g/7 oz each
10 ml/2 tsp runny honey
1 tbsp sea salt

Heat the olive oil in a medium saucepan and add the rice. Stir fry for a couple of minutes then mix in the tomato sauce, coating the rice well. Add the bouillon powder and some seasoning, then the boiling water. Give it one good stir, bring to the boil, cover the pan, turn the heat down to low and cook, undisturbed, for 50 minutes. Remove the lid and fluff it up gently with a fork. Cover with a dishcloth and the lid and set aside for 5 minutes.

While the rice is cooking, make the salsa first and then deal with the duck.

The coconut cream needs to be soft in order to give the salsa its lovely creamy consistency, so start off by either heating it very gently indeed in a small pan, or placing it in a glass or china bowl over a pan of simmering water. When the coconut cream is soft and malleable, place it with all the other ingredients except the peanuts and mango in a food processor and process until smooth. Add the peanuts and whizz it up for a few more seconds, just to break down the nuts without losing their texture. Season to taste. Scrape into a small bowl and add the mango. The salsa can be prepared up to a couple of hours in advance but after that it will start to lose its vivid green colour.

Heat the olive oil in a frying pan and sear the flesh side of the duck fillets on high heat for about 3 minutes. Remove them from the frying pan and place them skin side up in a small baking dish. Spread the honey over the skin and sprinkle evenly with sea salt.

Fifteen minutes before the rice is ready, heat the grill to high and grill the duck, skin side up and still in its baking dish, 10 cm/4 in from the heat for about 5 minutes, until the skin is dark and crisp. Test it for doneness by pressing it gently with your thumb – it should be firm but with a bit of bounce. Allow it to rest for 10 minutes then carve it on the diagonal into thin slices.

Scoop the rice on to a large serving dish and arrange the duck slices on top. Drizzle with some of the salsa.

Serve immediately, with extra salsa on the side.

MEXICAN *BOLOGNESE*
Picadillo

I couldn't think of a good translation for the name of this classic Mexican dish, but since it is in many ways reminiscent of the classic Italian dish, I settled for *bolognese*! I do actually often use it as a spaghetti sauce, and it is also very good in a shepherd's pie topped with a root vegetable mash – turnip or swede are both delicious – and in moussaka, or simply on its own with some rice. In Mexico, *picadillo* is used as a filling for *tacos, enchiladas, poblano* chillies, delectable puff pastry turnovers called *empanadas* (page 237), tortilla casseroles (page 84) – the variations are endless. You can also add some beans to it to make it into a Tex-Mex chilli. It is faintly sweet with raisins and spices, tangy from the roast tomato sauce, crunchy with almonds – in fact wonderfully savoury and reminiscent of the cuisines of northern Africa. Minced lamb is a good alternative to the pork, but beef somehow does not give it enough flavour.

30 g/1 ¼ oz whole blanched almonds
30 ml/2 tbsp olive oil
150 g/5 oz onions, peeled and coarsely chopped
2 garlic cloves, peeled and crushed
400 g/14 oz minced pork
1 tsp Mexican dried oregano (see Resources)
1 tsp cumin seeds
1/8 tsp ground cloves
½ tsp ground cinnamon
20 g/¾ oz raisins
½ x quantity Roast Tomato Sauce (page 204)
120 ml/4 fl oz water
Sea salt and freshly ground black pepper

Heat the oven to 160°C/300°F/gas 3/fan oven 145°C.

Place the almonds on a baking tray and cook them in the oven until golden, about 10 minutes. Cool and chop very coarsely.

Heat the olive oil in a large frying pan and fry the onions and garlic until soft and lightly browned, about 15 minutes. Add the pork and cook on low heat, stirring occasionally and breaking up any lumps with the back of a wooden spoon, until well browned – this will take 20 to 30 minutes and is very important to the final flavour of the dish. Crush the oregano and cumin seeds coarsely in a mortar or spice grinder and add to the pork, along with the cloves, cinnamon, raisins and some seasoning. Stir-fry for a minute then add the tomato sauce and the water. Mix well and cook for about 10 minutes longer so that the meat absorbs the flavour of the tomato and the sauce reduces a bit – you are aiming for a saucy but not runny consistency. Stir in the almonds.

Check the seasoning and serve immediately, or cool and refrigerate until ready to use.

PASTRY TURNOVERS
Empanadas de Picadillo

Tortilla turnovers are often referred to as *empanadas,* but since *pán* is Spanish for bread and wheat arrived with the Spaniards, an authentic *empanada* must surely involve wheat flour pastry... In Mexico, a type of puff pastry is used, but I prefer to make *empanadas* with filo pastry, as it is quicker and the result is lighter. The *empanadas* are eaten as a snack, rather than as part of a meal, and although they are delectable when hot as the pastry is crisp and crunchy, they make fabulous picnic food, particularly during a walk on a cold winter's day. A miniature version is also fantastic as a cocktail canapé.

Makes 10 *empanadas*

10 sheets filo pastry, approximately 45 cm/17 in x 25 cm/10 in
75 g/3 oz butter, melted
1 x quantity Picadillo (page 235), cooled

Lay a sheet of filo pastry out on the worktop, covering the remaining sheets with a damp dishcloth as filo dries out quickly. Brush the sheet with melted butter. Lay a second sheet on top of the first one and brush again with butter. With a sharp knife, cut the filo sheets lengthways into two long strips. Place 1/10 of the Picadillo about 5 cm/2 in from the end of each strip. Fold the 5 cm/2 in flap up and over the filling, bringing the left-hand corner across to the right to form a triangle; fold the triangle up and then over to the left, and continue up the strip, folding it like a flag, ensuring that the corners are neat and tight so that the filling does not ooze out during cooking. Repeat the procedure with the remaining filo pastry and Picadillo. Place the empanadas on a baking tray.

The empanadas can be prepared up to this point ahead of time and refrigerated or frozen. Defrost and bring back to room temperature before baking.

Heat the oven to 200°C/400°F/gas 6/fan oven180°C and bake the empanadas for about 20 minutes, until they are golden and crisp.

Serve immediately.

Papalotl

pod

Palenque

The temples and palaces of the ancient Mayas were adorned with stone carvings of a pod. The pod was a symbol of life and fertility and hidden inside it was the 'food of the gods': small, dark beans which were roasted and pounded, then made into a bitter drink, flavoured with chilli, herbs, vanilla or honey, to be consumed during religious ceremonies. The drink was sacred and divine, restricted to kings and lords, noblemen and high priests.

The Aztecs acquired the pod by trade and by sword. They prized it so highly that they considered it their greatest treasure – far greater than gold or silver – and used its beans as currency: a mere 100 beans was enough to buy a turkey or a slave, and even taxes and tribute were paid in beans. The pod also had a decidedly sinister religious use as the Aztec gods had an unquenchable thirst for blood and demanded constant human sacrifices: the palpitating heart would be torn from the chest of the victim, usually a prisoner of war, and offered up to the sky to propitiate the gods; a pod was then placed in the gaping, bleeding chest cavity...

When the Spaniards arrived at the court of Moctezuma, the great Aztec emperor, they were staggered by the gastronomic abundance and splendour of the imperial dining table, including the thick, cold, bitter liquid called *xocolatl*. 2000 jugs of it were served daily at court and Moctezuma himself is said to have drunk 50 golden goblets of chocolate every day, reckoning that the divine drink built resistance, fought fatigue, and enhanced sexual prowess.

I renewed my love affair with Mexican hot chocolate at a market *fonda* in Oaxaca. I sat on a tall stool at the counter and, in a haze of nostalgia, watched the cook as she heated some milk in a battered little saucepan. With a small *machete*, she hacked a chunk off a large block of chocolate wrapped in brown paper and dropped it into the hot milk. Then, rolling her little wooden *molinillo* between the palms of her hands, she whisked my *chocolate* until it was smooth and frothy. The taste brought tears of joy to my eyes.

On a later occasion, high in the Sierra Madre mountains of Michoacán, we watched a Tarasca Indian woman make chocolate by hand. With her baby strapped to her back in a *rebozo,* a brightly coloured striped shawl, she knelt on the bare earth of the village market place, roasting cocoa beans on a large cast iron griddle set over hot coals and stirring them with a bunch of twigs. She then heated a *metate,* a large smooth slab of volcanic rock traditionally used for grinding everything from corn for tortillas to roast tomatoes for a *salsa.* When it was hot – and you could tell it was hot by the strange stony smell – she ground the roast beans to a paste on it with a lump of lava shaped like a rudimentary rolling pin. As the crushed beans melted, she added coarse brown sugar, cinnamon and some flaked almonds. The air all around her was thick and velvety with the fragrance of warm chocolate and spices, so rich and mesmerising that I felt totally drugged – it wrapped itself around the onlookers like a soft, voluptuous cloak, drowning us in its magic folds.

When the chocolate mixture started to cool, the Tarasca *maître chocolatier* patted it into rough cakes with a wooden spatula, marked a cross on the tops with the tip of a knife and put them aside to set and harden. They were then piled up into stacks of five and wrapped in large squares of greaseproof paper.

I have never tasted chocolate like it – the flavour was pure, raw, spellbinding, remorselessly moreish and addictive. I lugged several packets of it around in my suitcase for the rest of the trip and all the way home, knowing that it would eventually keep homesickness at bay.

Mexican chocolate is slightly on the bitter side and flavoured with spices like cinnamon and vanilla; its texture is dense, faintly brittle and crunchy, coarser and grainier than the smooth, melting sophistication of modern chocolate. My favourite brand was called Carlos V after the Spanish monarch at the time of the Conquest, and it came in boxes of 20 bars wrapped in gold paper. I can still see it so clearly, lurking at the bottom of my lunch-box, under my *torta.*

Although I came across a savoury sauce flavoured with chocolate in Barcelona, Mexican cuisine is, to my knowledge, the only traditional one which uses chocolate in savoury dishes, essentially in sauces, and its role is similar to that of a spice. The flavour itself is elusive but it imparts a richness, a dark sultriness which is impossible to describe. *Mole Poblano* is arguably the national dish of Mexico, a wonderfully exuberant, special occasion concoction served at *fiestas* and celebrations: turkey is cooked in a deep and complex sauce, thickened with nuts, heavy with chilli and spices, sweet with raisins, and bitter with chocolate – eating it is a remarkably palate-expanding experience and well worth the labour intensive preparation.

Puddings are not the stars of a Mexican meal: fresh fruit, icecream or sorbet, *flán*, rice pudding, jelly. At simple restaurants, you will often be served a *dulce*, a "sweet", which is more confectionery and sweetmeat than proper pudding: crystallised fruit, fruit pastes, nut brittles, cream-filled pastry cones, even jam. Chocolate tends to be regarded as a morning drink, but when it does appear at the end of a meal, it is usually partnered with spices or tropical fruit. I have not so far found real Mexican chocolate in the UK, but Green & Black's Organic Maya Gold chocolate stirs up childhood memories and is a good substitute in sweet dishes. I have to admit that my puddings are rich to the point of excess – decidedly unfashionable by 21st century standards and definitely special occasion treats rather than every day fare.

MOLE

A real, proper Mexican *mole* is light years away from 21st century fast food. The list of ingredients is long, the instructions seem endless and just looking at a recipe can make one feel exhausted and washed out. *Mole* cookery requires a specific frame of mind, which is normally only available to me at weekends – it is a leisure activity, not to be entered into unless one is relaxed, with plenty of time available, and prepared to be fascinated and enthralled. In these circumstances, one is free to be drawn into the mystery and sorcery of an authentic *mole,* and the glory of its rich complexity of spice, fruitiness, bitter sweetness, underlying earthiness; and one can witness sheer alchemy, as seemingly totally disparate ingredients gradually fuse into a harmonious, balanced and indescribably delicious whole.

We were bitterly disappointed in the *moles* we ate in Mexico – alternately sweet and sickly, bitter, sometimes with no flavour other than searing heat, and invariably served lukewarm. It was only after our return home, when I started experimenting with *mole* in my own kitchen and researching it, that I realised why. *Mole* is *fiesta* food for Mexicans, and the *moles* served in restaurants are aimed at tourists and made with commercial *mole* pastes. They cannot possibly compare to a *mole* made at home, from scratch, with all the right ingredients.

The word *mole,* from the Nahuatl *molli,* actually means sauce, but stew or casserole is a rather more accurate description on the whole. It is thickened with seeds or nuts, and each region has its own version, based on its particular native chillies and what is grown locally. The most famous is the *Mole Poblano,* which features a turkey, and Oaxaca has no less than seven renowned and different coloured *moles* all to itself. Chocolate, however, does not feature in all *moles,* although it does in the two recipes below.

The first recipe is the more elaborate, the second one is more approachable, specially if you are new to *mole;* neither of them is truly authentic or the real thing, they would not be able to hold their heads up in Puebla or Oaxaca – but they are genuine enough to introduce you to the splendour and magic of Mexico's national dish. Both recipes benefit from being made a couple of days in advance, and freeze well, making them ideal for entertaining.

I always serve *mole* with plain rice garnished with fried plantains and a crunchy, fruity salad – see pages 250 and 252.

MOLE POBLANO

This recipe makes a lot of sauce, far more than you think you need. But one of the secrets of *mole* is to make sure the chicken – or turkey or pork – is completely immersed in the sauce so that it can become totally imbued with the flavour. Any left-over sauce can be frozen or served with fried eggs, stirred into basic beans, poured over roast potatoes, made into *enchiladas* (page 256); I even mix it with cooked penne or macaroni, top it all with grated cheese and bake it in the oven for 15 minutes – delectable. It is worth tasting the black, sinister-looking chilli purée on its own, just to experience its bitterness, its unadulterated heat (which is far from extreme), its surprising and strong suggestion of tobacco, and its overall fruitiness – prunes and dried figs in my opinion.

Serves 4

125 g/4 ½ oz mulato chillies (see Resources)
40 g/1 ½ oz ancho chillies (see Resources)
30 g/1 ¼ oz pasilla chillies (see Resources)
75 ml/5 tbsp olive oil
1 chicken, jointed into 8 pieces
50 g/2 oz sesame seeds
1 tsp cumin seeds
1 tsp coriander seeds
1 tsp fennel seeds
200 g/7 oz onions, peeled and coarsely chopped
2 garlic cloves, peeled and crushed
¼ tsp ground cloves
1 tsp ground cinnamon
30 g/1 ¼ oz sultanas
2 corn tortillas, torn into pieces
½ x quantity Roasted Tomatoes (page 205)
50 g/2 oz dry-roasted peanuts
500 ml/17 fl oz chicken stock, or water with 1 tsp bouillon powder
40 g/1 ½ oz dark chocolate (minimum 70% cocoa solids), broken into pieces
15 g/½ oz fresh coriander, coarsely chopped

Sea salt
Plain rice with plantains (page 250), to serve
Crunchy fruit salad (page 252), to serve

Heat a heavy frying pan over medium heat and toast the chillies, pressing down on them with a spatula, until they start to smell aromatic, about 3 minutes. Flip them over and do the same on the other side. Place them in a bowl, cover with boiling water, put a small saucepan lid or plate on top to keep them submerged, and set them aside to soak for 30 minutes. Drain them, discard the stems, seeds and ribs, and cut them into 2 cm/¾ in pieces. Place them in a food processor with 120 ml/4 fl oz of water and process until fairly smooth. Strain through a medium mesh sieve to remove the bits of skin. Set aside.

While the chillies are soaking, heat 30 ml/2 tbsp of the olive oil in a large frying pan or casserole and brown the chicken well all over. Remove the chicken to a plate to cool. Set the frying pan aside for use later.

Heat the heavy chilli frying pan again over medium heat and add the sesame, cumin, coriander and fennel seeds. Stir-fry them for about 5 minutes, until they are lightly browned and smell toasty. Cool and grind coarsely in a spice grinder or food processor. Set aside.

Heat the heavy frying pan for the third time, add the remaining 45 ml/3 tbsp of olive oil and cook the onions and garlic, stirring occasionally, until soft and golden, about 15 minutes. Add the cloves and cinnamon, sultanas and tortilla pieces, and cook for a further 5 minutes.

Place the tomatoes, peanuts, ground seeds, onion mixture and stock in a food processor and process until fairly smooth. Set aside.

All these steps can be done individually and ahead of time.

Put the frying pan or casserole in which you browned the chicken back on the heat and add the chilli purée. Cook for 10 minutes, stirring frequently, to thicken it. Add the tomato purée and cook for another 10 minutes, again until thick. Add the chocolate, cover and simmer very gently for one hour, stirring occasionally. Season and taste – if it is too sour or bitter, add a bit of sugar, just enough to balance the flavours. Add the chicken to the sauce, coat it well, cover the pan and simmer for another hour, until the chicken is tender.

Garnish with coriander and serve immediately with the rice and salad.

RED MOLE
Mole Rojo

Serves 4

30 ml/2 tbsp olive oil
500 g/18 oz stewing beef or pork, cubed
150 g/5 oz onions, peeled and coarsely chopped
2 garlic cloves, peeled and crushed
30 g/1 ¼ oz sultanas
1 tsp cumin seeds, coarsely crushed in a mortar or spice grinder
1 tsp ground cinnamon
¼ tsp ground cloves
1 x quantity Roast Tomato Sauce (page 204)
15 ml/1 tbsp chipotle chilli sauce (see Resources)
30 g/1 ¼ oz chopped, toasted hazelnuts, coarsely ground in a food processor or spice grinder
300 ml/½ pint water
15 g/½ oz dark chocolate (minimum 70% cocoa solids), broken into pieces
15 g/½ oz fresh coriander, coarsely chopped
Sea salt
Plain rice with plantains (page 250), to serve
Crunchy fruit salad (page 252), to serve

Heat 1 tbsp of olive oil in a heavy frying pan and brown the pork or beef well on all sides for about 10 minutes, stirring frequently. Remove to a plate and add the rest of the olive oil to the pan. Stir in the onions and garlic, and cook until soft and golden, about 15 minutes. Add the sultanas and spices and stir-fry for 1 minute, then add the tomato and chilli sauces, hazelnuts, water and chocolate. Bring to the boil, stir in the pork or beef, season, and simmer, covered, for one hour, until the meat is meltingly tender. Check the seasoning.

Sprinkle with coriander and serve immediately.

PLAIN RICE WITH PLANTAINS
Arroz con Plátano Macho

A classic accompaniment to a Mexican meal, from *mole* to *tacos,* or just often served by itself, as a course in its own right, and rather mystifyingly known as a *sopa seca,* "dry soup". A Mexican cook would not of course use brown rice, and the frying stage would involve very considerably more oil; our cook virtually "deep-fried" rice in a good inch of oil, and I can still remember its beautifully separate grains and light texture. Plantains – *plátano macho* or "male" banana – although not indigenous, are very popular throughout Latin America, and used solely in savoury dishes. They are quite firm and starchy, with a low sugar content, but frying or grilling brings out their very special flavour. They need to be fairly ripe so look for plantains with a yellow skin – or keep green ones for a week, even two, until they change from green to gold.

Serves 4

15 ml/1 tbsp olive oil
200 g/7 oz brown basmati rice
600 ml/1 pint boiling water
½ tsp sea salt
120 ml/4 fl oz vegetable oil
2 large, ripe plantains, about 250 g/9 oz each, peeled and sliced into
1 cm/½ in rounds

Heat the olive oil in a medium, heavy-bottomed saucepan and add the rice. Stir-fry for 1 minute to coat well, then add the salt and boiling water. Give it one good stir, cover the pan, turn the heat to low, and cook undisturbed for 50 minutes.

Fifteen minutes before the rice is ready, heat the oven to its lowest setting and put a large serving dish to warm. Heat the vegetable oil in a non-stick frying pan and add the plantain slices in one layer, browning them quickly on both sides – keep them moving around in the oil as they stick easily.

Remove to a baking tray lined with kitchen paper and keep warm in the oven.

When the rice is ready, fluff it up with a fork, tip it into the serving dish and garnish with the plantain slices.

Serve immediately.

CRUNCHY FRUITY SALAD

I particularly like a fruity salad with *mole*, and much Mexican food for that matter, as it interacts wonderfully with the chilli and chocolate flavours, cooling the heat and cleansing the palate. It also makes an excellent first course on its own, a refreshing, bright start to a meal. In Mexico, this kind of salad normally contains *jícama*, an indigenous tuber which tastes rather like a green apple. It is often available in ethnic food shops or large supermarkets, so if you can find one, peel it, cut it into slender sticks and add it to the salad.

Serves 4

2 large navel oranges
150 g/5 oz fennel, cored and finely sliced
1 medium red pepper, about 175 g/6 oz, cut into short, narrow strips
1 medium yellow pepper, about 175 g/6 oz, cut into short, narrow strips
1 red chilli, deseeded and finely sliced
50 g/2 oz red onions, peeled and finely sliced
60 ml/4 tbsp olive oil
1 large ripe avocado
100 g/4 oz rocket
15 g/½ oz mint, coarsely chopped
15 g/½ oz flat leaf parsley, coarsely chopped
Sea salt and freshly ground black pepper

Peel the oranges with a sharp knife, cut out the segments straight into a large salad bowl and squeeze the juice from the membrane on top of the oranges. Add the fennel, peppers, chilli, onions and olive oil and mix well. The salad may be prepared up to this point several hours ahead.

Shortly before serving, peel the avocado, remove the stone and cut into long slices about 1 cm / ½ in wide, then cut the slices in half. Add to the bowl with the rocket, herbs and some seasoning and toss gently.

Serve immediately.

PRAWN AND *CHIPOTLE* CHILLI *MASA* TARTLETS
Sopes de Camarón Enchipotlado

The menu at Patricia Quintana's glorious restaurant, Ixote, on Presidente Mazaryk in Mexico City, is complex and bewildering to the uninitiated – if you have little experience of Mexican food, it can be daunting. But the trick is to avoid trying to understand it all and jump straight in, in the knowledge that whatever you choose will expand your consciousness and enrich your life. Her focus is on pre-Hispanic food and although her cooking manages to be inexplicably rustic, authentic and sophisticated at the same time, a visit to Ixote will blow each and every single preconception you have ever had about Mexican food.

We chose the selection of hors d'oeuvres – *botanas* – to start with. These *sopes* – tartlets made of *masa*, cornmeal – were topped with juicy pink prawns in a warm, rich sauce spiked with smoky *chipotle* chilli. But there was something else, a hint of sweetness, an extra dimension, a deeper layer of flavour, which I just couldn't pin down. It was only hours later that it came to me in a flash: chocolate. When I played around with the idea in my own kitchen, I realised I was right. My sauce is simple: a basic roasted tomato sauce enhanced with *chipotle* and chocolate, which works wonderfully with the faint sweetness of the corn and the prawns.

If you do not have the time or inclination to make the *sopes*, the prawns in their sauce are just as good with plain tortilla chips.

Serves 2

For the sopes:-
65 g/2 ½ oz masa harina (see Resources)
15 g/½ oz wholemeal flour
10 g/1/3 oz butter, softened
¼ tsp salt
¼ tsp baking powder
85 ml/3 ¼ fl oz lukewarm water
1 tbsp olive oil
200 g/7 oz tomatoes, halved

1 tsp olive oil + 1 tbsp
65 g/2 ½ oz onions, peeled and coarsely chopped
1 garlic clove, peeled and crushed
½ tsp chipotle chilli sauce (see Resources)
10 g/1/3 oz dark chocolate (minimum 70% cocoa solids)
8 large raw king prawns, shelled and deveined
Soured cream or Greek-style plain yoghurt
Fresh coriander leaves
Sea salt and freshly ground black pepper

To make the sopes, place the masa harina, flour, butter, salt and baking powder in a food processor and process briefly. With the motor running, pour in the water and process until it is just amalgamated. Scrape into a bowl, knead into a ball, cover with clingfilm and set aside to rest for 30 minutes.

Heat the grill to high. Line the grill pan with foil and arrange the tomato halves on it, cut side up. Drizzle with1 tsp of olive oil and season well. Grill them about 5 cm/2 in from the heat until softened and starting to blacken around the edges, about 15 minutes.

While the tomatoes are cooking, heat the 1 tbsp of olive oil in a small frying pan, add the onions and garlic, and cook gently until soft and starting to brown, about 15 minutes. Tip them into the bowl of a food processor, add the tomatoes and their juices, and blend until fairly smooth. Return the mixture to the pan and cook for a few minutes, stirring, to evaporate any excess moisture – it should be nice and thick, but it will not take long as grilling the tomatoes dries them out quite considerably. Stir in the chipotle chilli sauce and chocolate, and cook until the chocolate has melted. Check the seasoning and add some more chilli sauce if it is not fiery enough for you. Set aside.

Heat the oven to its lowest temperature and put two plates to warm.

Divide the dough into 2 balls and flatten them into circles about ¾ cm/1/3 in thick. Heat a heavy, preferably non-stick, frying pan over medium heat, add the olive oil and cook the sopes for 3 to 4 minutes on each side until golden. With a spatula, transfer them to the two warm plates and carefully pinch the edges up with your thumb and index finger to form a tartlet case – don't worry if they are not perfect, it really doesn't matter! Return them to the oven to keep warm while you cook the prawns.

Reheat the tomato sauce to simmering point, add the prawns and cook them over medium heat, stirring, until they just turn pink. Divide the prawn mixture between the two sopes, and top with a good spoonful of sour cream or yoghurt and some coriander leaves.

Serve immediately.

Cacao

CHICKEN AND *MOLE* ENCHILADAS
Enchiladas de Mole

This is a perfect dish for using up frozen left-over *mole* sauce, cold chicken from the Sunday roast, and odds and ends of cheese which have been cluttering up the refrigerator for a couple of weeks – which is why I do not give exact quantities.

Although we were deeply disappointed in the *moles* we ate in Mexico – particularly since *mole* is virtually the national dish – the colourful Los Colorines Restaurant in Tepoztlán bucks the modern trend of using commercially prepared *mole* pastes and hand-makes its own *mole* the traditional way. The serving kitchen, so Mexican with its decorative tiling and bright pink walls, opens out into the restaurant, and the lovely cook, an absolute picture in her starched white apron and her hair tucked into a white lace *coiffe*, stands behind her big terracotta pans of simmering, aromatic sauces. She reacted to my interest and queries with a warm smile and explained to me in detail the characteristics of each dish. When I told her of my overall disappointment in *mole*, she promised me that if I tried her enchiladas, my faith would be restored and my stomach gladdened. She was right, they were deeply flavoured, rich and savoury, utterly satisfying, Mexican cooking at its brightest and best – and just what we needed after our arduous climb up the rocky mountain path and past the stupendous crags to the temple of Tepoztecatl, the rabbit god of fertility.

Mole sauce – leftover is ideal for this (pages 18, 246 and 249)
Corn tortillas
Cooked, shredded chicken
Farmhouse Cheddar cheese, coarsely grated
Soured cream or Greek-style plain yoghurt
Fresh coriander leaves
White onion, peeled and finely sliced

Heat the sauce in a frying pan large enough to hold a tortilla. With kitchen tongs, dip a tortilla into it, making sure both sides are coated with sauce. Transfer the tortilla to one end of a china baking dish. Fill it with some chicken and fold it over. Repeat the process with all the tortillas, lining them up in the dish side by side and slightly overlapping them.

When they are all done, pour the remaining sauce over the enchiladas and wrap the dish securely in foil.

Heat the oven to 200ºC/400ºF/Gas 6/fan oven 180ºC and bake the enchiladas for about 15 minutes, until piping hot. Remove the foil, drizzle some soured cream or yoghurt over the top, and sprinkle liberally with grated cheese, coriander and sliced onions.

Serve immediately.

STEAK WITH CHILLI SAUCE
Bistec con Mole y Rajas

At first glance, this dish has strong Moorish associations, being flavoured with raisins, pine nuts and fresh coriander. But the first mouthful takes you right back to Mexico with the warm, savoury richness of the chillies and chocolate. You can't actually taste the chocolate, but try making the sauce without it and you will realise what a huge contribution it makes. In Mexico, we were served rice as an accompaniment, and although I had never considered rice an appropriate partner to a steak, it works well. But feel free to be more traditional and eat it with chips!

Serves 2

20 g/¾ oz pine nuts
500 g/18 oz tomatoes, halved
1 x quantity Multicoloured Rajas (page 103)
1 tsp ground cinnamon
20 g/¾ oz raisins
5 ml/1 tsp olive oil
2 steaks
15 g/½ oz dark chocolate (minimum 70% cocoa solids), coarsely chopped
15 g/½ oz flat leaf parsley, coarsely chopped
Sea salt and freshly ground black pepper

Heat the oven to 160°C/325°F/gas 3/fan oven 145°C. Place the pine nuts on a baking tray and bake them until golden, 7 to 10 minutes. Set aside to cool.

Heat the grill to high. Line the grill pan with foil, arrange the tomatoes cut side up on it, season well and grill 5 cm/2 in from the heat for about 15 minutes, until softened and lightly charred. Process them in a food processor until fairly smooth.

Place the rajas in a heavy medium saucepan and sprinkle with cinnamon. Stir-fry over medium heat for a minute or two, then add the tomato purée and raisins. Turn the heat right down and leave to simmer while you cook the steaks.

Brush a ridged cast-iron griddle or frying pan with the olive oil and heat it until really hot. Season the steaks and cook them for about 3 minutes on each side for rare, 5 minutes for medium. Transfer them to two warm plates.

Sprinkle the chocolate over the sauce, stir for a few seconds to melt it, and add the pine nuts and parsley.

Spoon some sauce over the steaks and serve immediately, with the rest of the sauce on the side.

MEXICAN HOT CHOCOLATE WITH *CHURROS*
Chocolate con Churros

Christmas without *chocolate con churros* for breakfast could never be Christmas for me – even nowadays. We were lucky enough to live at one time near Elizondo, the most fashionable and very stylish bakery-cum-pâtisserie in Mexico City in those days, and its *churros* were sublime – the housemaid was often sent off to buy them on the spur of the moment, for pudding on a school day. But on Christmas Day, our cook would make them for us before going off to her native village, her *tierra*, for her annual holiday. *Churros* are deep-fried strips of choux pastry, flavoured with cinnamon – crisp and crunchy with sugar on the outside, soft and melting on the inside, decidedly European and nothing whatsoever to do with pre-Hispanic Mexican food! Hot chocolate with milk or cream is of course a mixture of New and Old Worlds, as it was made with just water before the arrival of the Spaniards – and having tried *chocolate pre-hispánico* on a couple of occasions and found it lacking in comfort, I always make my hot chocolate at home with milk and at least some cream.

HOT CHOCOLATE

Serves 2

250 ml/8 fl oz full cream milk
250 ml/8 fl oz single cream
100 g/4 oz Green & Black's Maya Gold chocolate
2 cinnamon sticks (optional)

Heat the milk and cream in a small saucepan until steaming. Remove from the heat, add the chocolate and whisk until melted. Pour into two cups and garnish with a cinnamon stick.

Serve with churros.

CHURROS

Makes about 10 churros

150 g/5 oz plain flour
½ tsp + 1 tsp ground cinnamon
250 ml/8 fl oz water
100 g/4 oz unsalted butter
Pinch of salt
3 eggs
1 litre/1 ¾ pints vegetable oil
30 g/1 ¼ oz caster sugar

Sift the flour with the ½ tsp cinnamon. Bring the water, butter and salt to the boil in a heavy, medium saucepan. Add the flour all in one go and stir vigorously until the dough forms a mass and comes away from the sides of the saucepan. Remove from the heat and beat the eggs in, one at a time. Scoop the dough into a piping bag fitted with a fluted nozzle and leave to cool for about one hour (a disposable plastic piping bag, available at cookware shops, is ideal).

Heat the oil in a large frying pan or deep-fat fryer to 190°C/375°F. Pipe the dough straight into the hot oil in 15 cm/6 in lengths, cutting it away from the nozzle with scissors. Cook about 4 at a time, depending on the size of your frying pan, until they are golden, then turn them over and cook the underside – about 3 to 5 minutes on each side. Remove them with a slotted spoon or spatula to a baking tray lined with kitchen paper.

When all the churros are cooked, mix the sugar and remaining cinnamon in a roasting tin, add the churros and shake them around gently, spooning the sugar over them, until they are well coated and nice and crunchy.

Serve immediately while they are still slightly warm, with a mug of steaming hot chocolate.

The churros are also very nice cold although their texture becomes less light as they cool.

Churros con chocolate

CHOCOLATE SANDWICH
Torta de Chocolate

A Mexican version of *pain au chocolat* in many ways. My best friend used to bring this *torta* to school in her snack box – but then her parents were second generation Belgians which perhaps explains their imaginative use of chocolate. On the other hand, we came across chocolate sandwiches in a number of bakeries during our trip, so there must be something Mexican to the idea, perhaps a creation of the Emperor Maximilian's Austrian pastry chef. We often take a chocolate *torta* on long winter walks; they are quick to make, delicious and unquestionably sustaining. The textures are wonderful and a delight to bite into: crisp crust, soft crumb, hard chocolate, melting moments.

Makes 2 sandwiches

2 small crusty rolls
Butter, softened
30 g/1 ¼ oz Green & Black Maya Gold chocolate, broken into pieces

Split the rolls and spread them liberally with butter. Arrange the chocolate down the middle of the bottom halves and cover with the top halves.

Eat immediately or wrap tightly in clingfilm if you are going to transport them anywhere.

MEXICAN CHOCOLATE ICECREAM
Helado de Chocolate

Green & Black's Maya Gold chocolate is the best for this recipe, as it is the only chocolate I have found which gives the icecream the elusive spiciness of the real Mexican thing. I have also tried making it with plain bitter chocolate, and adding some cinnamon, or infusing a vanilla pod with the milk and cream, both of which work well, so don't be put off if you can't find Maya Gold or prefer a purer, more intense chocolate flavour. This is gloriously rich icecream, as only home-made icecream can be, so I serve it in smallish portions. The *polvorones* on page 275 go very well indeed with it.

Serves 8

250 ml/8 fl oz full cream milk
500 ml/17 fl oz double cream
125 g/4 ½ oz caster sugar
6 egg yolks
200 g/7 oz Green & Black's Maya Gold chocolate, broken into pieces

Heat the milk and cream in a medium saucepan until steaming.

Place the sugar and egg yolks in a large bowl and whisk at high speed with an electric beater until thick and pale. Reduce the speed to low and carefully whisk in the hot milk and cream. Return the mixture to the saucepan and cook over low heat, stirring constantly with a wooden spatula, until it thickens to a custard consistency and coats the spatula – be careful not to overheat it or it will curdle. Remove from the heat and add the chocolate, stirring until it melts and the custard is totally smooth. Pour into a clean bowl and cool completely.

Refrigerate until really cold and churn in an icecream machine. Store in a plastic container in the freezer.

CHOCOLATE CUSTARD
Flán de Chocolate

I loathed *flán* when I was a child. I hated its resilient, bouncy texture and the bitterness of the caramel. My mother made it out of a packet – I don't ever remember our cooks making puddings except for the Christmas *churros* – and it was served regularly. *Crème caramel* will never be one of my favourites, even when it is properly made, but I did come across a very light, chocolate version on several occasions during our visit; the texture was almost milk and chocolate jelly which did not enthral me, but the flavour was lovely. Jelly vendors are a common sight in Mexican towns, positioning themselves at the entrances to markets and bus stations to pick up all the passing trade. Their wares are a pretty and colourful sight, artistically displayed in glass cases: wobbly, shimmering, bright green lizards, scarlet castles, striped blancmanges, acid yellow pineapples.

My chocolate *flán* is more of a chocolate cream because I prefer a custard with a dense consistency; it does not turn out of a mould particularly well, so I tend to set and serve it in a ramekin, with a thin chocolate crust and a dusting of cocoa. It is hopelessly rich and incredibly moreish.

Makes 2 x 120 ml/4 fl oz/½ cup ramekins

75 ml/2 ¾ fl oz full cream milk
175 ml/6 fl oz double cream
2 egg yolks
2 tbsp caster sugar
150 g/5 oz Green & Black's Maya Gold chocolate, broken into pieces
½ tsp cocoa powder

Heat the milk and cream in a medium saucepan until steaming.

Place the egg yolks and sugar in a large bowl and whisk at high speed with an electric beater until thick. Reduce the heat to low and carefully whisk in the hot milk and cream. Return the mixture to the saucepan and cook over low heat, stirring constantly with a wooden spatula, until it thickens to a custard consistency and coats the spatula – be careful not to overheat it or it will curdle. Remove immediately from the heat, add 125 g of the chocolate and stir until melted and totally smooth. Pour into the ramekins – a jug makes this easier – cool, and refrigerate overnight.

Melt the remaining 25 g/1 oz of chocolate in a small bowl over very hot but not boiling water, then drizzle it over the top of the custards and smooth it right to the edges with the back of a teaspoon. Refrigerate again until ready to serve.

Use a fine mesh sieve to dust the tops with cocoa powder just before taking them to the table.

CHOCOLATE RICE PUDDING
Arroz con Leche y Chocolate

Rice pudding is incredibly popular in Mexico – it is often part of *comidas corridas* (set menus) in restaurants, and comes heavily flavoured with vanilla, cinnamon and citrus peel, never quite creamy enough for my liking but fragrant and pleasantly spicy. We had a chocolate version in a rather expensive, modern, *nouvelle cuisine* type restaurant in Mexico City which was recommended by a school friend and turned out to be exactly the kind of restaurant which we try to avoid – but the rice pudding was divine. I like Arborio risotto rice in rice pudding – it is a nice big grain which holds its shape well and has plenty of starch to thicken the pudding to a velvety consistency.

Serves 6

175 g/6 oz risotto rice
500 ml/17 fl oz full cream milk
350 ml/12 fl oz double cream
50 g/2 oz unsalted butter
75 g/3 oz caster sugar
100 g/4 oz Green & Black's Maya Gold chocolate, broken into pieces
1 x 1-litre/1 ¾ pint baking dish
Double cream, to serve (optional but good!)

Put the rice, milk and cream in a saucepan and bring very gently to the boil, stirring occasionally. Cover the pan and leave to simmer for 10 minutes. Remove from the heat and stir in the butter and sugar. Cool slightly, then mix in the chocolate.

Heat the oven to 150°C/300°F/gas 2/fan oven 135°C. Pour the rice pudding into the baking dish, cover with foil, and cook for 40 minutes. Remove the foil and cook for a further 10 minutes, until a slight skin has formed over the top.

Serve immediately with plenty of cold double cream.

VANILLA ICECREAM WITH HOT CHOCOLATE SAUCE
Helado de Vainilla con Salsa de Chocolate

Acapulco – brash, brassy, Americanised heaven, where we always spent our two week winter holiday (too rainy in summer). Every day followed the same blissful pattern: water-skiing before breakfast, down to the beach for the morning, back to the hotel for lunch, siesta and then the beach again until late afternoon. A quick shower, a fancy holiday outfit, and off to the coast road promenade to join the crowds of glamorous holiday makers; perhaps a visit to the mini-golf, dinner at Dino's, and definitely an icecream, either at the Dairy Queen or Tastee-Freeze. Tastee-Freeze was by far my favourite, because they did the best chocolate sauce, thick, glistening, mysterious. Looking back on it, it probably came from a squeezy bottle, but I adored it. I prefer to use a rich, dark, bitter chocolate for my sauce, to set off the exoticism of real vanilla and the sweetness of the icecream.

VANILLA ICECREAM

Serves 6

2 vanilla pods
250 ml/8 fl oz full cream milk
500 ml/17 fl oz double cream
6 egg yolks
125 g/4 ½ oz caster sugar
1 x quantity Hot Chocolate Sauce (page 269)
30 g/1 ¼ oz chopped, toasted hazelnuts

Split the vanilla pods lengthways and scrape the seeds out with the tip of a knife into a medium saucepan. Add the pods, milk and cream and heat gently, stirring occasionally, until steaming.

Place the egg yolks and sugar in a large bowl and whisk with an electric beater on high speed until thick and pale. Reduce the speed to low and carefully whisk in the hot milk and cream. Return the mixture to the saucepan and cook gently, stirring all the time with a wooden spatula, until it thickens to a custard consistency and coats the spatula – be careful not to overheat it or it will curdle. Pour into a clean bowl and allow to cool completely, then refrigerate until really cold. Remove the vanilla pods and churn in an icecream machine. Store in a plastic container in the freezer.

To serve, place a scoop of icecream in individual bowls or coupes, pour over some chocolate sauce and garnish with hazelnuts.

Serve immediately. It will all melt and blend into a wonderful chocolate and vanilla goo.

HOT CHOCOLATE SAUCE

Serves 6

500 ml/17 fl oz double cream
30 g/1 ¼ oz unsalted butter
200 g/7 oz dark chocolate (minimum 70% cocoa solids), broken into
small pieces

Heat the double cream in a small saucepan until steaming. Remove from the heat and add the butter and chocolate, stirring until totally melted and smooth. Use immediately.

CHOCOLATE AND COCONUT TART WITH COCONUT ICECREAM
Pai de Coco y Chocolate con Helado de Coco

Coconut and chocolate make a happy couple, as I found at a fancy restaurant on the Caribbean coast, where scoops of coconut and chocolate icecreams were served in a coconut shell – a very dramatic presentation. But the idea for this tart came from some chewy, moist pastry squares which I found very early one morning in a *panadería* – bread shop – near the Palenque bus station. We had a nine hour bus ride ahead of us, down from the highlands of Chiapas and across the Yucatán peninsula to Mérida, and needed some sustenance for the trip. Although *panadería* translates literally as bread shop, they are a cross between a bread shop and a *pâtisserie,* with great big metal trays in the windows laden with meringues, biscuits, tartlets, cakes, and the typical sweet breads which every Mexican has for breakfast with a cup of hot chocolate or strong coffee – the Emperor Maximilian's most delicious legacy.

CHOCOLATE AND COCONUT TART

Serves 10

For the pastry:-
425 g/15 oz plain flour
1 tsp salt
50 g/2 oz caster sugar
225 g/8 oz unsalted butter, very cold, cut into pieces
2 egg yolks, lightly beaten
50 ml/2 fl oz cold water
1 x 27 cm/11 in metal tart tin with a removable base

For the filling:-
200 g/7 oz unsweetened, dessicated coconut
4 eggs
250 g/9 oz light brown sugar
40 g/1 ½ oz unsalted butter, melted
400 g/14 oz runny honey
200 g/7 oz dark chocolate (minimum 70% cocoa solids), coarsely chopped

For the pastry, place the flour, salt, sugar and butter in a food processor and process until the mixture resembles fine crumbs. With the motor running, add the egg yolks and water, and process until it just holds together. Turn the pastry out onto a floured work surface, knead lightly with the heel of your hand, flatten into a thick disk and place in a freezer bag. Refrigerate until firm, at least one hour. Remove from the refrigerator and roll out on a floured work surface to a 2 mm/ 1/10 in thickness. Carefully lift into the tart tin, gently mould into the bottom and sides, trim the edges, and freeze for at least 30 minutes.

Heat the oven to 200°C/400°F/gas 6/fan oven 180°. Prick the base of the pastry case with a fork, line with a large piece of foil (ensuring the edges are covered all the way round), fill with baking beans, and bake on a baking tray for 15 minutes. Remove the foil and beans and cook for a further 10 minutes. Cool.

To make the filling, heat the oven to 140°C/275°F/gas 1/fan oven 125°C. Spread the coconut on a baking tray and toast for 10 minutes, stirring once or twice, until light gold and aromatic. Cool.

Heat the oven to 180°C/350°F/gas 4/fan oven 160°C.

Sprinkle the chopped chocolate over the cooked pastry base. Whisk the eggs, sugar, melted butter, honey and toasted coconut in a bowl and pour over the chocolate. Place the tart on a baking tray and bake for about 40 minutes, until the filling is firm and the top lightly browned. Check it after 20 minutes and if the pastry is browning too much, protect the top of the tart with foil.

Allow the tart to rest for 15 minutes before removing from the tin and slicing.

Serve with coconut icecream.

COCONUT ICECREAM

Serves 10

150 g/5 oz unsweetened, dessicated coconut
350 ml/12 fl oz milk
350 ml/12 fl oz double cream
6 egg yolks
150 g/5 oz caster sugar

Heat the oven to 140°C/275°F/gas 1/fan oven 125°C. Spread the coconut on a baking tray and toast for 10 minutes, stirring once or twice, until light gold and aromatic.

Heat the milk and cream in a medium saucepan until steaming. Add the coconut and set aside to steep for one hour, then strain through a fine mesh sieve into a bowl, pressing down on the coconut with the back of a spoon to extract all the liquid and flavour. Discard the coconut. Rinse out the pan and pour in the milk and cream. Reheat to steaming.

Place the egg yolks and caster sugar in a large bowl and whisk with an electric beater on high speed until thick and pale. Reduce the speed to low and carefully whisk in the hot milk and cream. Return the mixture to the saucepan and cook gently, stirring constantly with a wooden spatula, until it thickens to a custard consistency and coats the back of the spatula – be careful not to overheat or it will curdle. Pour into a clean bowl and cool completely, then refrigerate until really cold.

Churn in an icecream machine and store in a plastic container in the freezer.

CARAMEL AND CHOCOLATE BREAD PUDDING
Pastel de Cajeta y Chocolate

When chatting to a Mexican friend living in England about Mexican food, she reminded me about a bread pudding traditionally served at Christmas – she remembered it from her childhood and it definitely rang a bell with me. She was not able to find a recipe for it but from her description and our joint reminiscences, it was a bread pudding flavoured with *cajeta*, a wonderful caramelised goat's milk concoction, as Mexican as you can get. My subsequent research came up with *capirotada* or *budín de pán* – bread pudding – which is obviously a close relative, but not the dish I recall. In this recipe, I am using a caramel sauce and chocolate. My friend thinks that slices of sponge cake were used but I like croissants in a bread pudding – not very Mexican, you may think, but *cuernos* – horns – are one of the Emperor Maximilian's contributions to the Mexican way of life.

Serves 8

For the caramel sauce:-
250 g/9 oz caster sugar
100 ml/3 ½ fl oz water
750 ml/1 ¼ pints double cream

For the pudding:-
6 croissants, sliced in half
75 g/3 oz sultanas
75 g/3 oz chopped, toasted pecans or hazelnuts
100 g/4 oz Green & Black's Maya Gold chocolate, broken into pieces
3 eggs
300 ml/½ pint full cream milk
1 tbsp icing sugar
1 x 1-litre/1 ¾ pint high-sided round baking dish

Start off with the caramel sauce. Put the sugar and water in a small, heavy bottomed saucepan and bring to the boil, stirring all the time to dissolve the sugar. Boil, without stirring, until it turns a rich gold – watch it like a hawk towards the end as it will burn in the blink of an eye. Remove from the heat and carefully pour in the double cream – it will hiss and splutter so stand well back (rubber gloves are a real asset here!). Return the pan to the heat and stir until the sauce is totally smooth. Cool.

Place half the croissants in the bottom of the baking dish. Sprinkle with the sultanas, nuts and chocolate. Cover with the remaining croissants, cut side up – they will create a natural, swirled pattern on the finished pudding. Whisk the eggs, milk and caramel sauce together in a bowl and pour over the croissants. Cover the dish with foil and set aside for at least 2 hours or, even better, refrigerate overnight.

Heat the oven to 150°C/300°F/gas 2/fan oven 135°C. Bake the pudding for 40 minutes, then remove the foil and bake for a further 20 minutes, until firm and lightly browned. Set aside for 10 minutes.

Dust with icing sugar just before serving.

Cuernos

CHOCOLATE AND ICING SUGAR BISCUITS
Polvorones de Chocolate

Proper *pâtisserie* came to Mexico with the Emperor Maximilian and his wife Carlota, whose entourage included a Viennese pastry chef, and the wide variety of sweet breads and biscuits, served particularly at breakfast, is one of the most enduring gifts that their short reign brought to Mexican cuisine. *Polvo* means dust and *Polvorones*, thickly dusted with icing sugar, come wrapped in brightly coloured tissue paper, rather like the Italian *amaretti*. Elizondo, an elegant and fashionable *pâtisserie* in Mexico City, made wonderful *polvorones* full of chocolate chips and nuts, and we always bought a big bag of them to take on long car journeys.

Makes 16 *polvorones*

50 g/2 oz toasted, chopped hazelnuts
90 g/3 ½ oz unsalted butter, softened
65 g/2 ½ oz caster sugar
Pinch of salt
1 egg yolk
1 tsp ground cinnamon
150 g/5 oz plain flour
75 g/3 oz plain chocolate (52% cocoa solids), coarsely chopped
Icing sugar

Place the hazelnuts in a food processor and grind them quite finely. Add the butter and sugar and process until light and creamy. Scrape down the sides of the bowl well, add the salt, egg yolk and cinnamon and process again until well mixed. With the speed on low, add the flour by the spoonful and process just until you have a homogenous mixture. Add the chocolate and process again briefly to distribute it evenly. Transfer the dough to a bowl and knead it lightly with the heel of your hand. Chill for 20 minutes as this will make the dough easier to handle and roll.

Heat the oven to 180°C/350°F/gas 4/fan oven 160°C and line a couple of baking trays with baking parchment. Roll the dough into balls the size of a walnut and arrange them 2 cm/¾ in apart on the baking trays. Bake for 20 minutes, until lightly golden. Cool for 5 minutes.

Put about 50 g/2 oz of icing sugar into a bowl and gently roll the *polvorones* around in it, coating them well. Add more icing sugar as necessary. Place the biscuits on a rack until completely cool and store in an airtight container.

CHOCOLATE *TAMALES*
Tamales Dulces con Chocolate

These sweet tamales took me totally by surprise, because I had never come across them flavoured with chocolate before – nuts, cinnamon and raisins certainly, but never chocolate. We bought them from a street vendor in arty Sán Miguel Allende and ate them sitting on a sunny bench in the main square; they were piping hot and the chocolate was all soft, gooey and quite wonderful. I have added cocoa powder to the *masa* base to enhance the chocolate flavour that much more. Savoury tamales are traditionally wrapped either in corn husks, or in banana leaves, but sweet tamales require the corn husks, as banana leaves add a flavour all of their own to the *masa* which suits chilli, meat and vegetables very well but not sugar, sweet spices or chocolate – unless of course you are cooking bananas in them (page 279).

Makes 8 tamales

100 g/4 oz corn husks (see Resources)
75 g/3 oz butter, softened
40 g/1 ½ oz caster sugar
½ tsp baking powder
1 tbsp cocoa powder
250 g/9 oz masa harina (see Resources)
400 ml/14 fl oz warm water
75 g/3 oz plain chocolate (52% cocoa solids), coarsely chopped
20 g/¾ oz chopped, toasted hazelnuts
2 tbsp soft dark brown sugar
15 g/½ oz sultanas
String (optional)
Double cream, to serve

Put the corn husks in a large bowl and pour a kettle of boiling water over them. Place a small saucepan lid on top to keep them submerged and leave them to soften and rehydrate for a couple of hours or even overnight.

Place the butter, caster sugar and baking and cocoa powders in a food processor and process until creamy and well blended. Add about ¼ of the masa harina followed by ¼ of the water, processing in between and repeating the procedure with the remaining masa harina and water until you have a thick batter.

Stir the chocolate, nuts, brown sugar and sultanas together in a small bowl.

Drain the corn husks, lay them out on a dishcloth, cover them with a second dishcloth, and pat them dry. Arrange enough of them on the work surface to make a square about 15 cm/6 in x 15 cm/6 in, overlapping several pieces of husk if necessary. Spread 1/8 of the batter on the square, leaving a 2 cm/¾ in border. Spoon 1/8 of the chocolate mixture in the centre of the batter. Fold one side of the corn husks up and over the batter and the filling, enclosing it all completely, then fold up the other side in the same way and tuck the ends under, to make a parcel. Don't worry if it is not particularly tidy, that is what tamales look like! Carefully pick the parcel up and set it aside, seam side down. Repeat with the rest of the batter and filling.

When the tamales are all made, they can either be steamed as they are, seam side down, or you can tie them up like a present, which makes them slightly easier to handle once they are cooked and improves the presentation. In Mexico, strips of cornhusk are used, which looks very ethnic and natural – but this also adds to the fiddliness of making tamales, so I use string.

Line a steamer with cornhusks or baking parchment and put it in a large saucepan with 3 cm/1 ¼ in of boiling water. Arrange the parcels in the steamer, cover the saucepan, and steam the tamales for 1 hour and 30 minutes. Check the level of the water every now and then and top up if necessary.

To serve, place one or two tamales on each plate and provide a pair of scissors to cut the string. Offer the cream separately.

Any leftover cornhusks can be left to dry out completely and used on another occasion.

BAKED BANANAS
Plátanos Asados

Grilled bananas would be a better description – the cook in the market in Mérida cooked them on an open grill high above a brazier of glowing hot coals. The wrapping of banana leaves protected them from the searing heat and added a hint of exoticism, a wisp of a flavour impossible to pin down. She served them to us in deep plates to make sure that the delicious juices would not be lost when we opened the packets. The banana leaves had turned brown and leathery, and as we pulled them back, we almost drowned in the intoxicating aroma of citrus, warm chocolate and soft, buttery bananas.

Frozen banana leaves are often available in ethnic supermarkets, but I have taken the easy route and cook the bananas in gratin dishes in the oven – not quite the same but still incredibly good, and infinitely more practical.

Serves 2

2 large bananas, peeled and sliced into 1 cm/½ in rounds
30 g/1 ¼ oz unsalted butter
15 g/½ oz caster sugar
Grated rind and juice of 1 medium orange
50 g/2 oz dark chocolate (minimum 70% cocoa solids), broken into
small pieces
¼ tsp ground cinnamon
2 x 12 cm/4 ½ in china gratin dishes

Heat the oven to 200°C/400°F/Gas 6/fan oven 180°C.

Divide the bananas between the two gratin dishes.

Melt the butter in a small saucepan, add the sugar and orange rind and juice, and bring to the boil. Stir in the cinnamon and pour it over the bananas. Sprinkle the chocolate on top. Wrap the dishes well in foil and bake them in the oven for 10 minutes.

Carefully unwrap the dishes and serve immediately – the bananas will be soft, the butter syrupy and bubbling, and the chocolate melted to a heavenly, gooey mess.

FRENCH TOAST
Pán Francés

Las Mañanitas in Cuernavaca is named after the Mexican birthday song (infinitely more romantic and evocative than Happy Birthday!) and is a truly wonderful boutique hotel, a peaceful, green sanctuary in the middle of what used to be a charming, laid-back provincial town and has now become a traffic-clogged, bewilderingly noisy, industrial city. Meals are served on the terrace at the edge of the lush gardens, under large green umbrellas. *Pán Francés* translates as French bread, but the version at *Las Mañanitas* is a cross between French Toast (or egg bread as it is sometimes called) and cinnamon toast, making it crisp and crunchy with cinnamon sugar, but with a soft, eggy interior. The hint of chocolate from the cocoa powder makes it more into Mexican Toast than French Toast.

Serves 2

1 egg
Pinch of salt
75 ml/2 ½ fl oz milk
2 thick slices soft bread
30 g/1 ¼ oz caster sugar
2 tbsp unsweetened cocoa powder
¼ tsp ground cinnamon
A knob of butter

Beat the egg with the salt and milk in a small bowl and pour it into a wide shallow plate or baking dish in which the two slices of bread will fit side by side. Place the bread in it and leave it to soak for 5 minutes, then turn it over with a spatula to soak on the other side.

While the bread is soaking, mix the sugar, cocoa and cinnamon in a plate.

Heat the butter in a non-stick frying pan over medium heat until frothy. Lift the bread with a spatula and place it in the frying pan. Cook for about 4 minutes on each side, until lightly browned. Remove it from the frying pan and place it in the sugar plate, pressing down lightly to coat it well. Flip it over carefully and do the same on the other side. Lift the slices onto two warm plates and sprinkle any remaining sugar mixture over the top.

Serve immediately.

WARM CHOCOLATE SOUFFLÉS WITH CINNAMON ICECREAM
Soufflé de Chocolate con Helado de Canela

La Michoacana is a chain of icecream shops, found in every town, however small. It was recommended by friends as being the best – and safest! – place to sample real Mexican icecream. It is certainly good icecream and comes in a baffling choice of flavours. But commercially produced icecream, whatever its quality, can never compare to that made by hand, and having decided to take a risk, we nervously sat down under an awning at an icecream stall in a leafy square in Oaxaca and watched the owners and their young daughter churn their icecreams by hand. The churns were set in large plastic trays packed with ice, and they cranked the handles with seemingly infinite energy and vigour. They were all delighted at my obvious interest and admiration, and told me that the bases for the icecreams were made at home every morning, and then turned into icecream at the stall. It was hard work to start with, they said, but as the mixtures became colder and started to freeze, they did not have to be churned quite so regularly. They had thirty different icecreams and sorbets – rather charmingly known as *nieves*, snows – on offer, and the ten we tasted between us were quite wonderful – very light as milk rather than cream is used, beautifully fresh and clean tasting, and yet deeply flavoured.

These chocolate "soufflés" are decidedly *nouvelle cuisine*, appearing on the menus of the more expensive restaurants we visited, and usually served with either cinnamon or vanilla icecream. They are not classical soufflés but soft and tender, with a liquid, molten heart – chocolate alchemy at its most seductive. They rise up nicely and develop a delicious crust to contrast with the luscious, squidgy interior, rather like a chocolate fondant. Timing is crucial, as 2 or 3 minutes of overcooking will set the centres and make them a bit solid, so be sure to remove them from the oven while they still have some wobble to them.

Serves 2

2 x 200ml/7fl oz china ramekins
Soft butter and sugar for coating the ramekins
75 g/3 oz dark chocolate (minimum 70% cocoa solids), broken into small pieces
75 g/3 oz unsalted butter

2 eggs
75 g/3 oz caster sugar
2 tbsp self-raising flour
1 tbsp icing sugar

Smear some soft butter all over the inside of the ramekins and sprinkle with sugar, twirling the ramekins to distribute it evenly.

Melt the chocolate and butter in a small bowl over very hot but not boiling water. Cool slightly.

Heat the oven to 200°C/400°F/Gas 6/fan oven 180°C.

Whisk the eggs, sugar and flour in a medium bowl. Gently stir in the cooled chocolate mixture and pour into the ramekins. Place the ramekins on a baking tray and bake for 20 minutes, until they are just set but the middle is still wobbly and the tops start to crack.

Sprinkle with icing sugar and serve immediately with cinnamon icecream.

CINNAMON ICECREAM

Serves 2

120 ml/4 fl oz double cream
1 egg yolk
25 g/1 oz caster sugar
¼ tsp ground cinnamon

Heat the cream in a medium saucepan until steaming.

Whisk the egg yolk, sugar and cinnamon in a bowl with an electric beater on high speed until thick and pale. Reduce the speed to low and slowly pour on the hot cream, whisking all the time. Return the mixture to the pan and cook over low heat, stirring constantly with a wooden spatula, until it thickens to a custard consistency and coats the spatula – be careful not to let it boil or it will curdle. Pour into a clean bowl and leave to cool completely, then refrigerate until really cold.

Churn in an icecream machine and store in a plastic container in the freezer.

RESOURCES

Chillipepperpete.com has an extensive range of dried and fresh chillies as well as Mexican oregano, pickles, relishes and sauces, condiments and spices. He grows his own fresh chillies in summer, including *jalapeños, serranos* and *poblanos*. His mixed chilli multipack is excellent for experimenting. 01273 705606, pete@chillipepperpete.com, www.chillipepperpete.com

Coolchile.co.uk supply Mexican *chorizos,* dried chillies, dried Mexican herbs, including oregano, epazote, hoja santa and avocado leaves, masa harina, fresh vacuum-packed tortillas, tortilla presses, corn husks, annatto seeds, chipotle chilli sauce; fresh *tomatillos* and chillies such as *serrano* and *poblano* are regularly, but not always, available. Some of their products, such as masa harina and chipotle chilli sauce, can be found in the speciality or "world foods" sections of large supermarkets. 0870 9021145, orders@coolchile.co.uk, www.coolchile.co.uk

Peppers by Post grow fresh chillies, *tomatillos* and the Mexican herb *epazote,* which are available by mail order during the summer months. 01308 897766, info@peppersbypost.biz, www.peppersbypost.biz

Seasoned Pioneers stock some dried Mexican chillies as well as annatto seeds and organic spices. 0800 0682348, feedback@seasonedpioneers.co.uk, www.seasonedpioneers.co.uk

Organic *tomatillo* seeds are available from The Organic Gardening Catalogue, 0845 1301304, www.organiccatalogue.com, enquiries@chaseorganics.co.uk

The Chocolate Alchemist makes fabulous plain dark chocolate with 73% cocoa solids. 01798 860995, info@thechocolatealchemist.com, www.thechocolatealchemist.com

INDEX

Illustrations

Lamb

Health Psychology

Process and applications

Second edition

Edited by

Annabel Broome

Annabel Broome Associates,
Weymouth, UK

and

Sue Llewelyn

University of Edinburgh,
Edinburgh, UK

CHAPMAN & HALL

London · Glasgow · Weinheim · New York · Tokyo · Melbourne · Madras

Published by Chapman & Hall, 2-6 Boundary Row, London SE1 8HN, UK

Chapman & Hall, 2-6 Boundary Row, London SE1 8HN, UK

Blackie Academic & Professional, Wester Cleddens Road, Bishopbriggs, Glasgow G64 2NZ, UK

Chapman & Hall GmbH, Pappelallee 3, 69469 Weinheim, Germany

Chapman & Hall USA., One Penn Plaza, 41st Floor, New York, NY10119, USA

Chapman & Hall Japan, ITP-Japan, Kyowa Building, 3F, 2-2-1 Hirakawacho, Chiyoda-ku, Tokyo 102, Japan

Chapman & Hall Australia, Thomas Nelson Australia, 102 Dodds Street, South Melbourne, Victoria 3205, Australia

Chapman & Hall India, R. Seshadri, 32 Second Main Road, CIT East, Madras 600 035, India

Distributed in the USA and Canada by Singular Publishing Group Inc., 4284 41st Street, San Diego, California 92105

First edition 1989
Reprinted 1991, 1992, 1993
Second edition 1995
Reprinted 1995

© 1989, 1995 Chapman & Hall

Typeset in 10½/12½ pt Sabon by EXPO Holdings, Malaysia
Printed in Great Britain by Clays Ltd, St Ives plc

ISBN 0 412 55120 9   1 56593 3226 9 (USA)

A Catalogue record for this book is available from the British Library

Library of Congress Cataloging-in-Publication Data available

∞ Printed on permanent acid-free text paper, manufactured in accordance with ANSI/NISO Z39.48-1992 and ANSI/NISO Z39.48-1984 (Permanence of Paper).